ANCIENT HAWAIIAN LEGENDS AND VINTAGE ILLUSTRATIONS, AN ADULT COLORING BOOK

by
Stephen Jorgensen

published by
CyberSuccess Publishing
Honolulu, Hawaii

This Adult coloring book has wonderful Hawaiian illustrated images for you to color. In the past, (late 1800's and early 1900's) pen and ink and woodcut illustration reached reached it's peak in creativity and simple design elegance. This was before photo lithography printing corrupted the art with mass reproduced photographs. So publishers were willing to pay well for popular talented artists that could draw illustrations that would really attract the public with their quality designs and so the art of illustration flowered. For this book, I have tried to make similar examples of these wonderful illustrations for this coloring book presentation. These illustrations are my own drawings done in the manner of vintage Illustrated Romantic and Fairy Tale books because there are just not enough real Hawaiian vintage illustrations available.

These designs are for colorists that just want to complete elegant designs. This artist has done other coloring books but he specializes in bigger Hawaiian paintings. All the works included here are by the Hawaiian artist Stephen E Jorgensen. He has over 200 other works of beautiful Hawaiian art available on his Etsy website. Most of his work is large canvas wall hangings, some of which are reduced to coloring pages for his Relaxing Hawaiian Scenes Coloring books. See these artworks at hawaiiseascapes.etsy.com.

I have colored-in samples of these vintage illustrations to show what they could look like and have printed the full color pictures on the front and back covers. Of course you are free to chose your own colors. Most of the images are outlines of recognizable objects or figures, so you should be able to just color in the spaces to fit what the object is without just following the picture example. Have fun coloring your Hawaiian Vintage Illustrations!

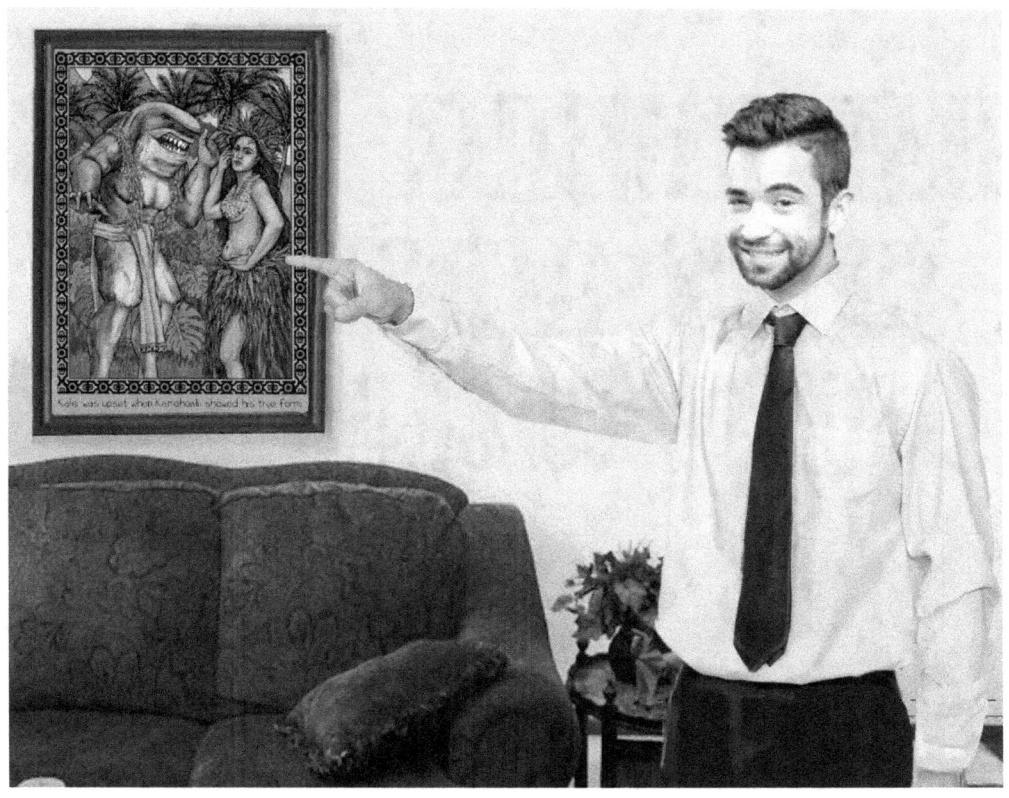

Feel free to make copies of the pages you are working on so you can try different coloring schemes. If you develop one that you really like, you can order a large poster sized coloring pages from our web site at Etsy. hawaiiseascapes.etsy.com and then make your own poster art. They come in 11" X 17" and 17" X 22" and 24" X 36" sizes.

ANCIENT HAWAIIAN LEGENDS AND VINTAGE ILLUSTRATIONS AN ADULT COLORING BOOK

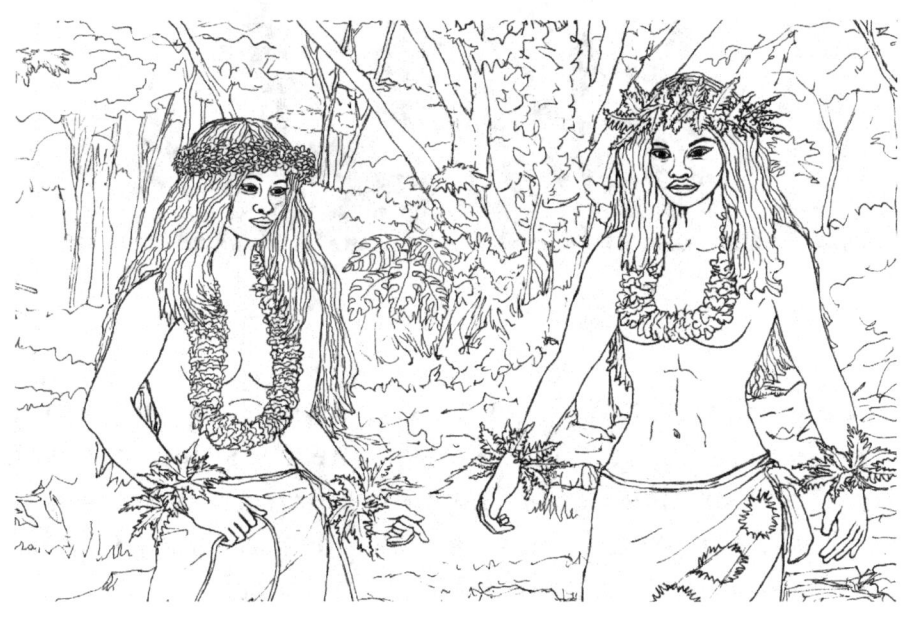

ISBN-13: 978-1979480574

ISBN-10: 1979480575

Copyright © S.E. Jorgensen 2017

ANCIENT HAWAIIAN LEGENDS AND VINTAGE ILLUSTRATIONS AN ADULT COLORING BOOK

The designs here are from old Hawaiian legends, some often very obscure, but some are well known tales. They are good for pleasant coloring fun even if you don't know the story behind them. You don't have to use the same colors I used on the images on the covers but those images will perhaps give you ideas.

If you do shading of the shapes then many of the colors are just slightly different, so it is best to used a large selection of colored pencils to be able to find an appropriate color, and it helps to "layer" two different colors to get a better match. For instance, coloring a purple over a red will give a darker more scarlet red.

All the coloring pages are one side only, so there will be no bleed-through that will mess up a drawing on the opposite side of the page if you do use color marking pens.

Enjoy your coloring. Relax, don't think too much, just color.

**This Vintage Coloring Therapy
will relax you. It is fun.**

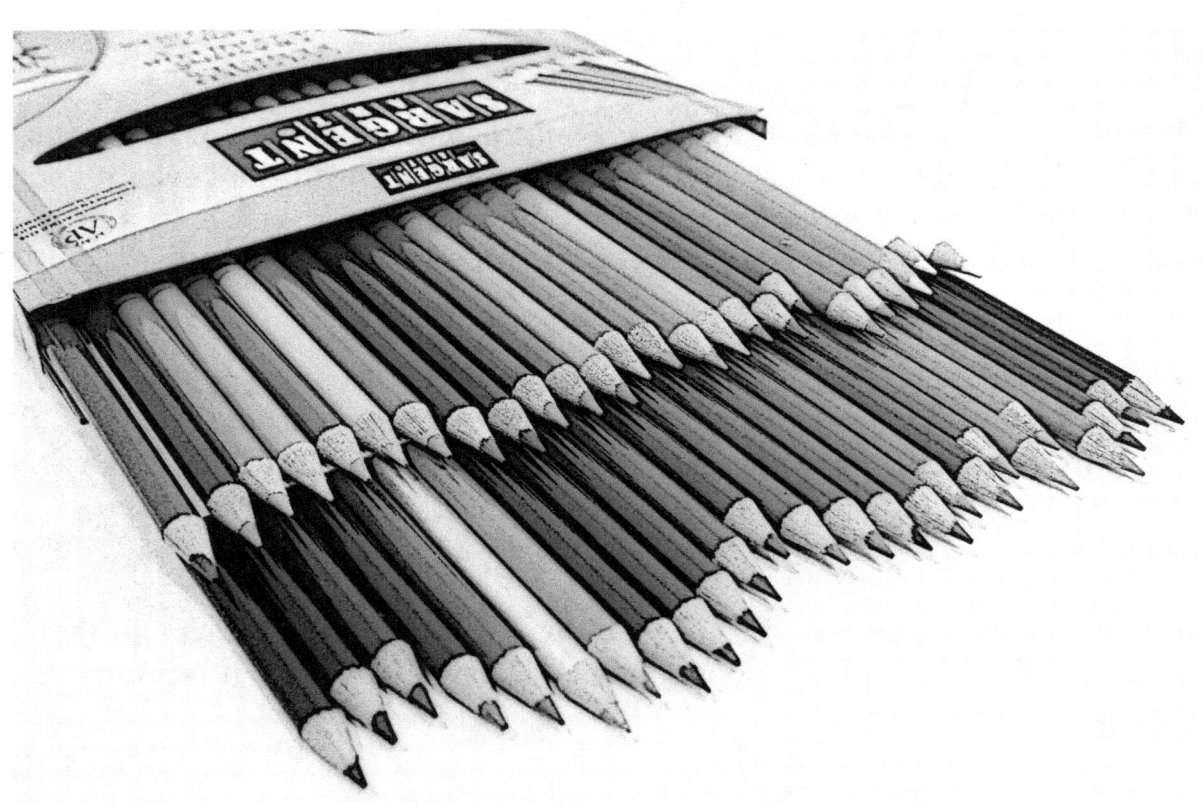

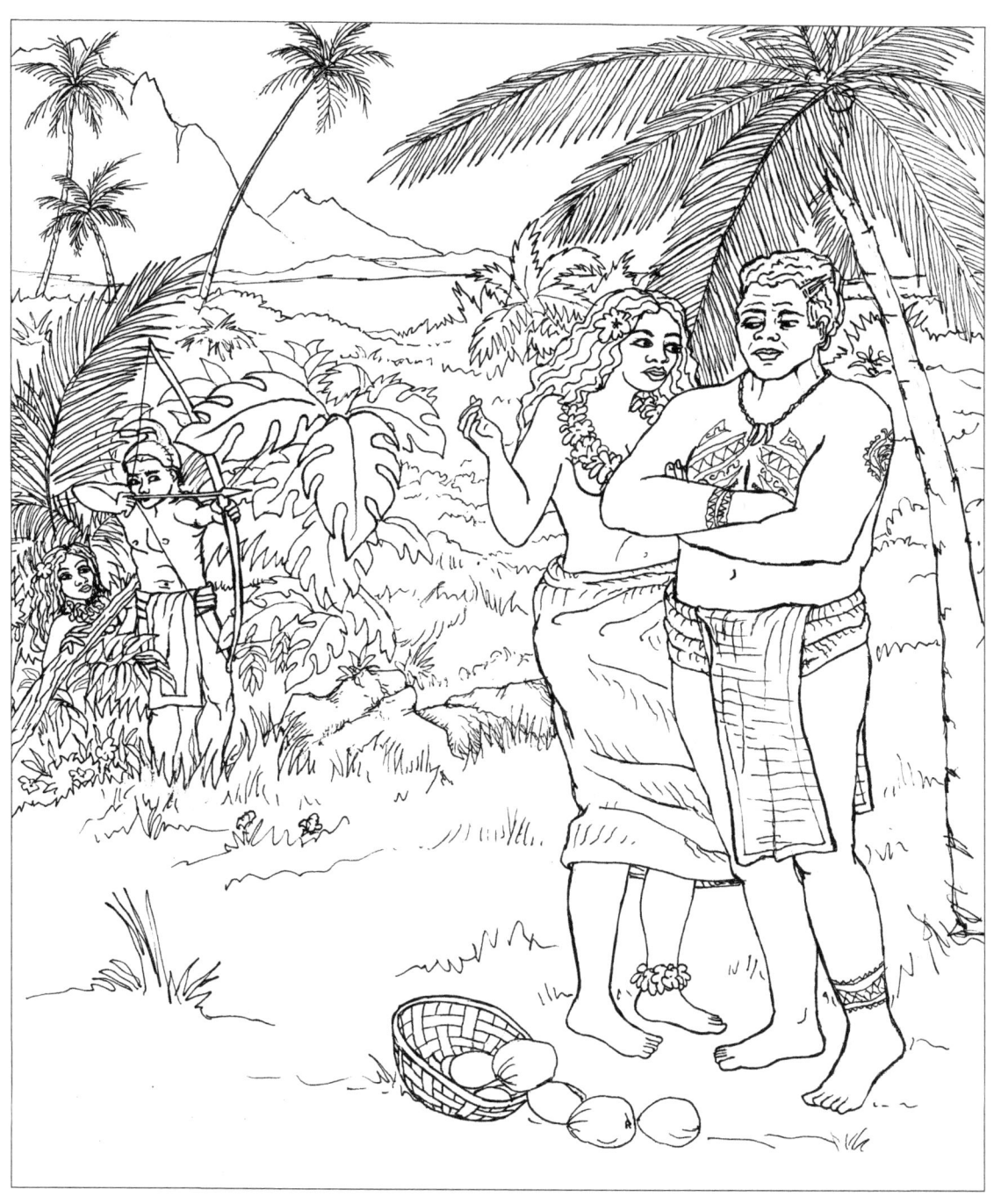

A Menehune aims an arrow of Love.

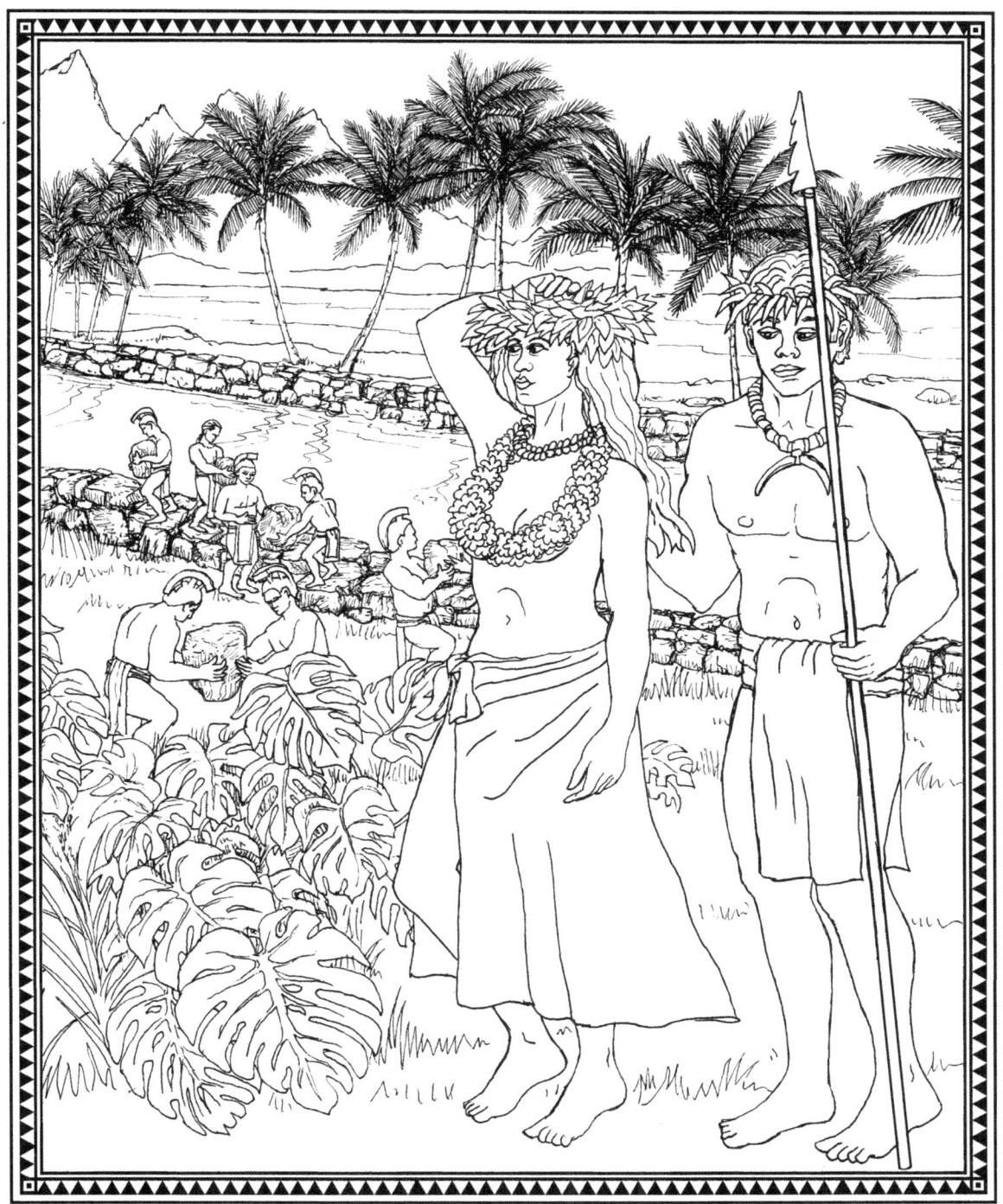
Menehune build Alekoko Fishpond for a princess and her brother.

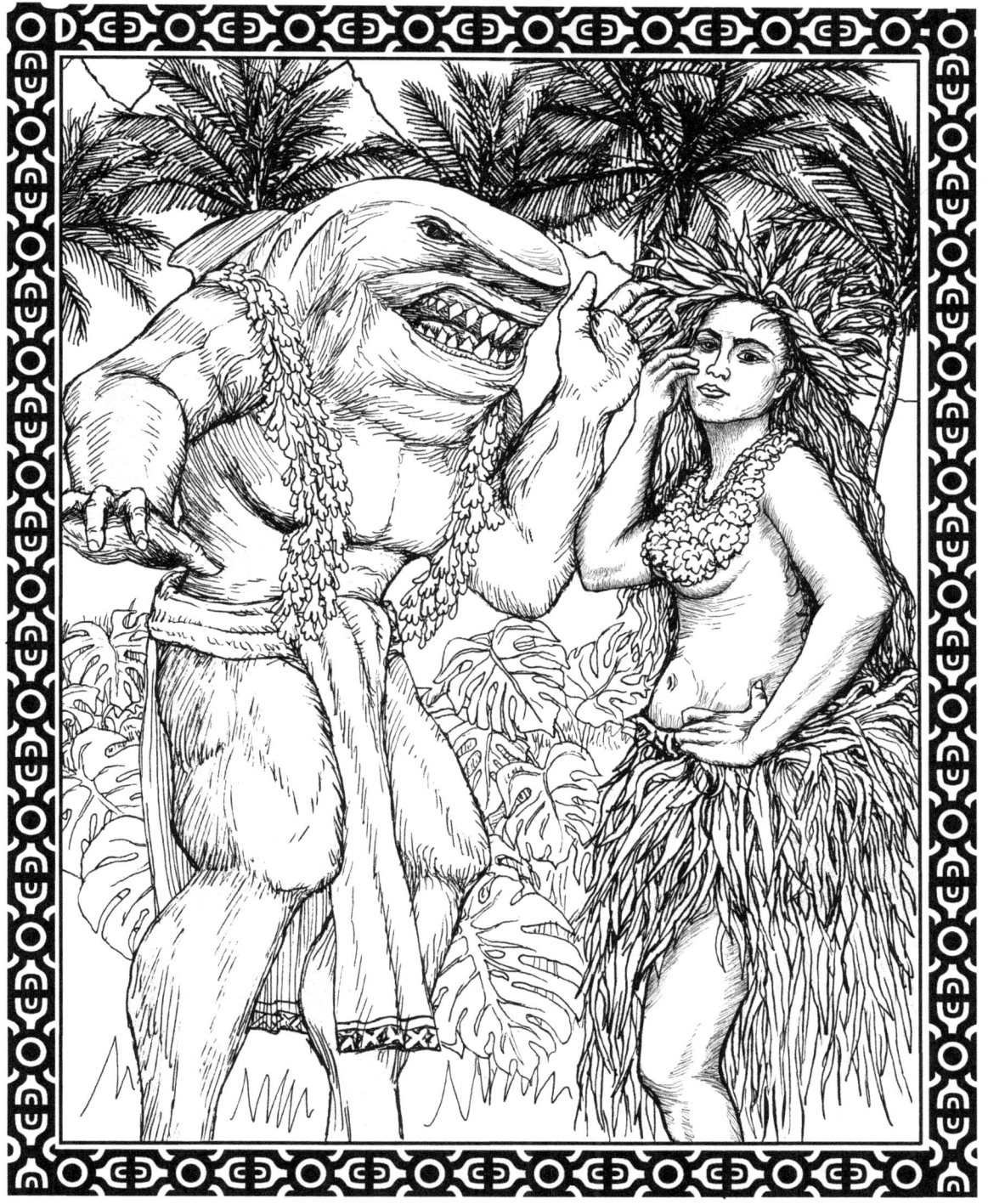
Kalei was upset when Kamohoalii showed his true form.

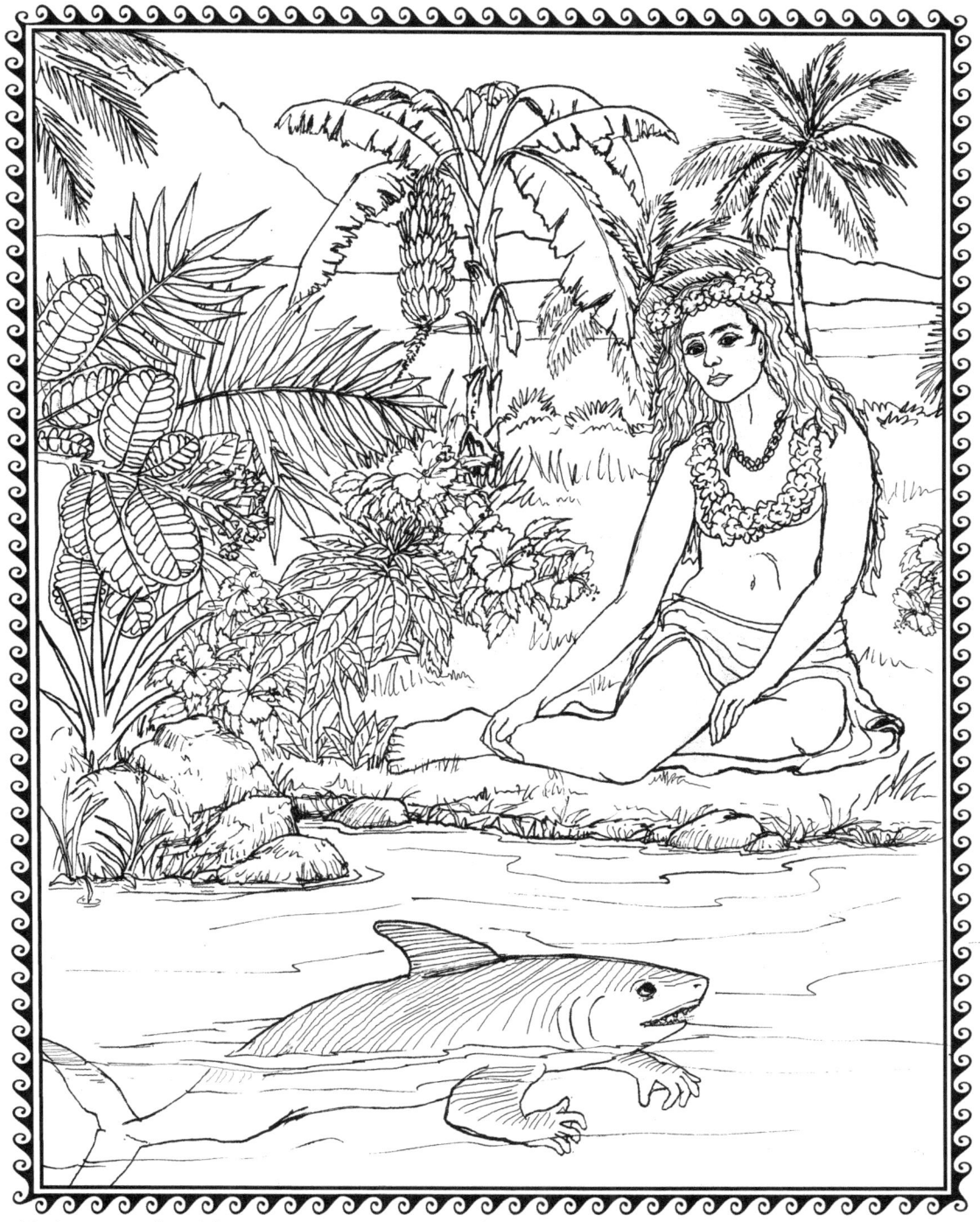
Kalei watched her son turn into a shark when they went to the stream.

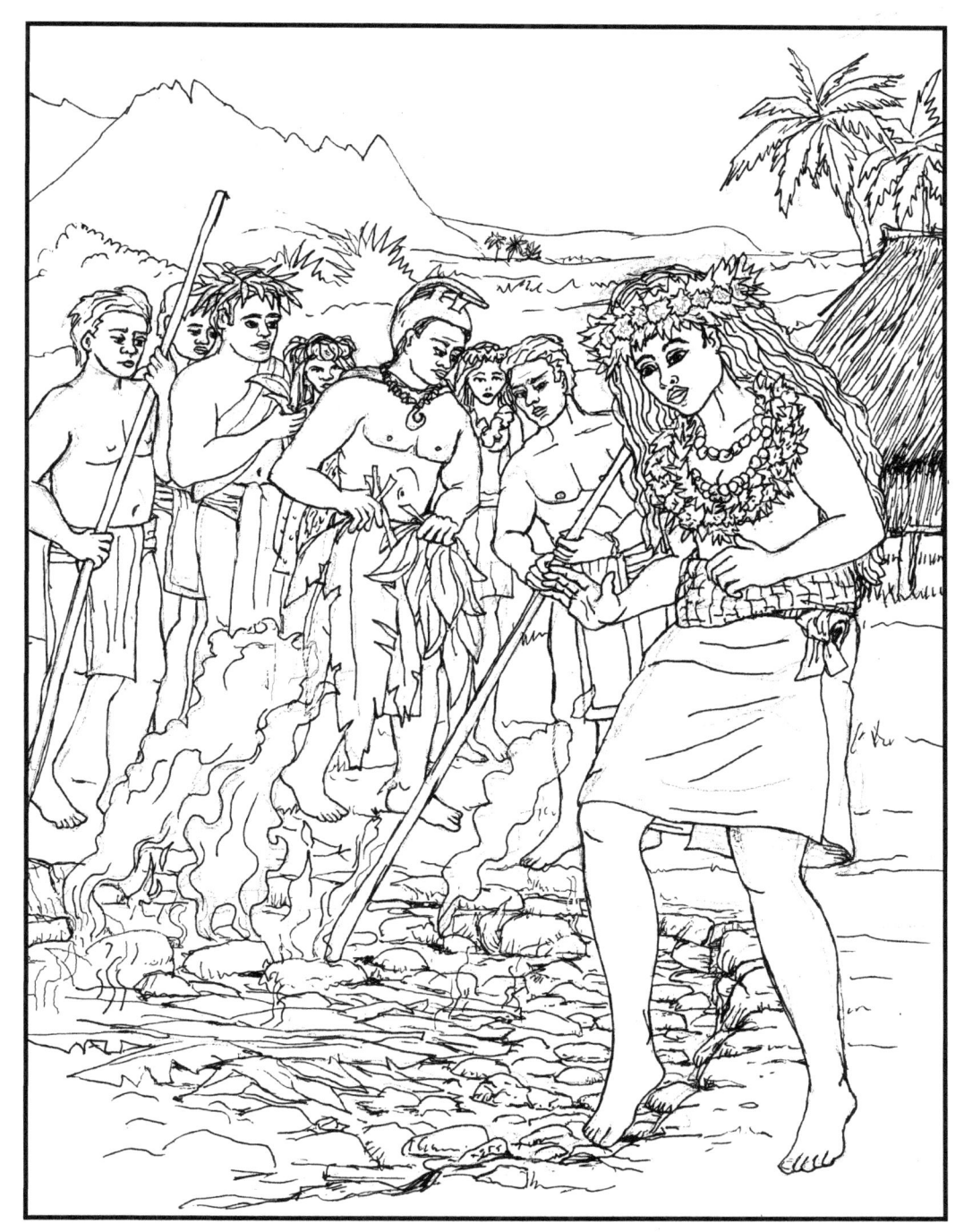

Hina Keahi stepped into the imu she had her people build.

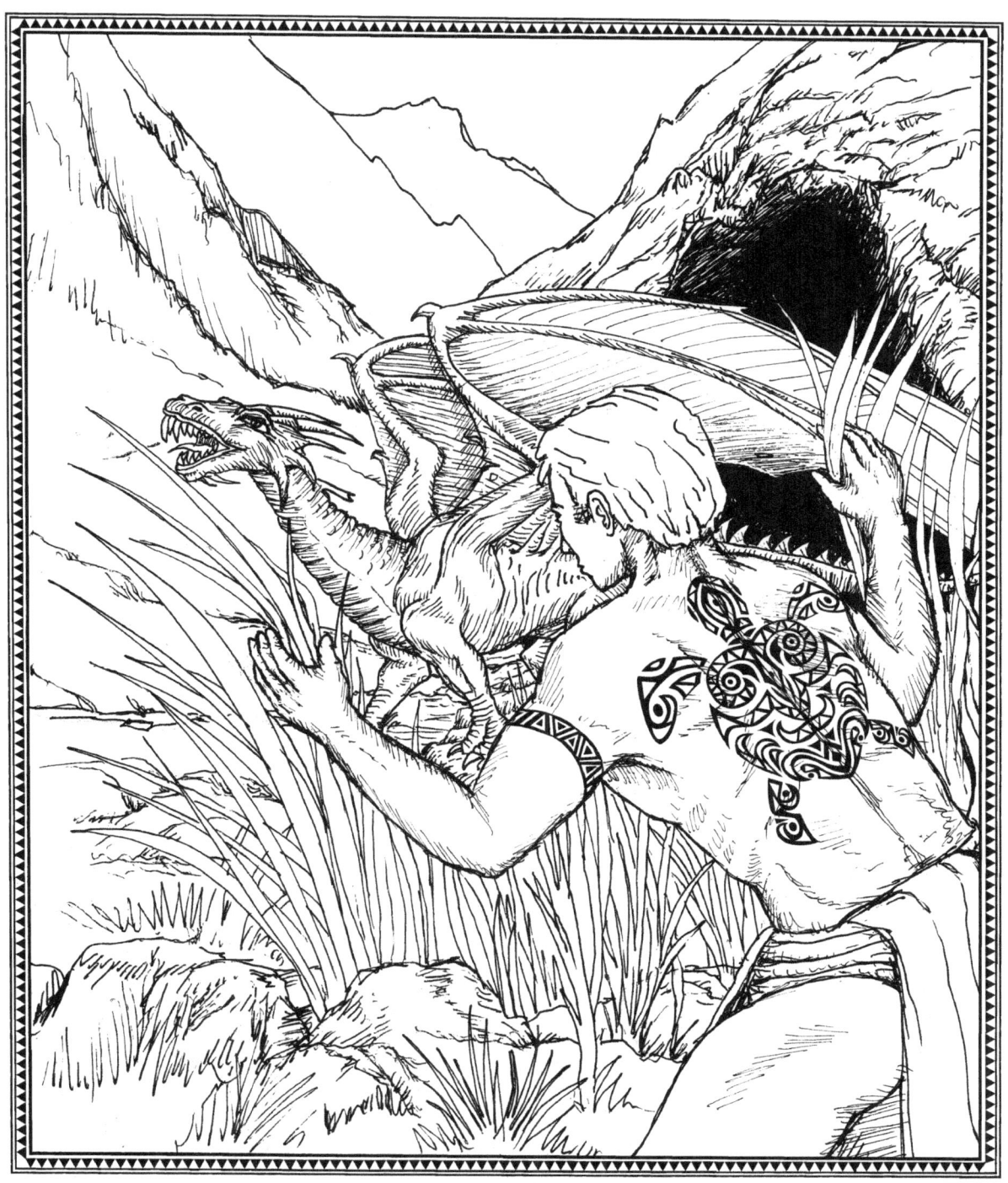
Sneaking up on the cave, he saw Kihawahine in her true form.

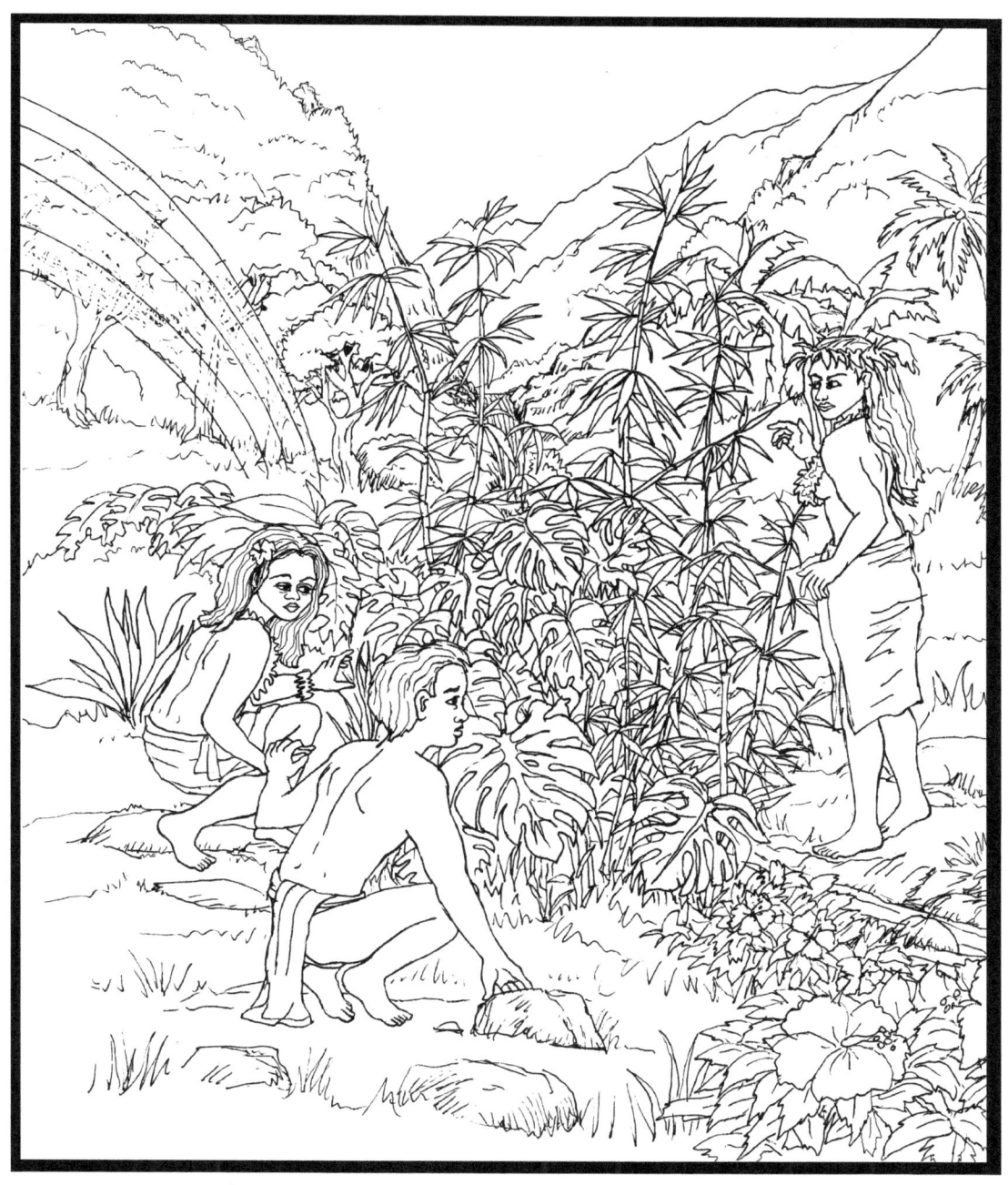

Hawea searching for her step children in Manoa valley.

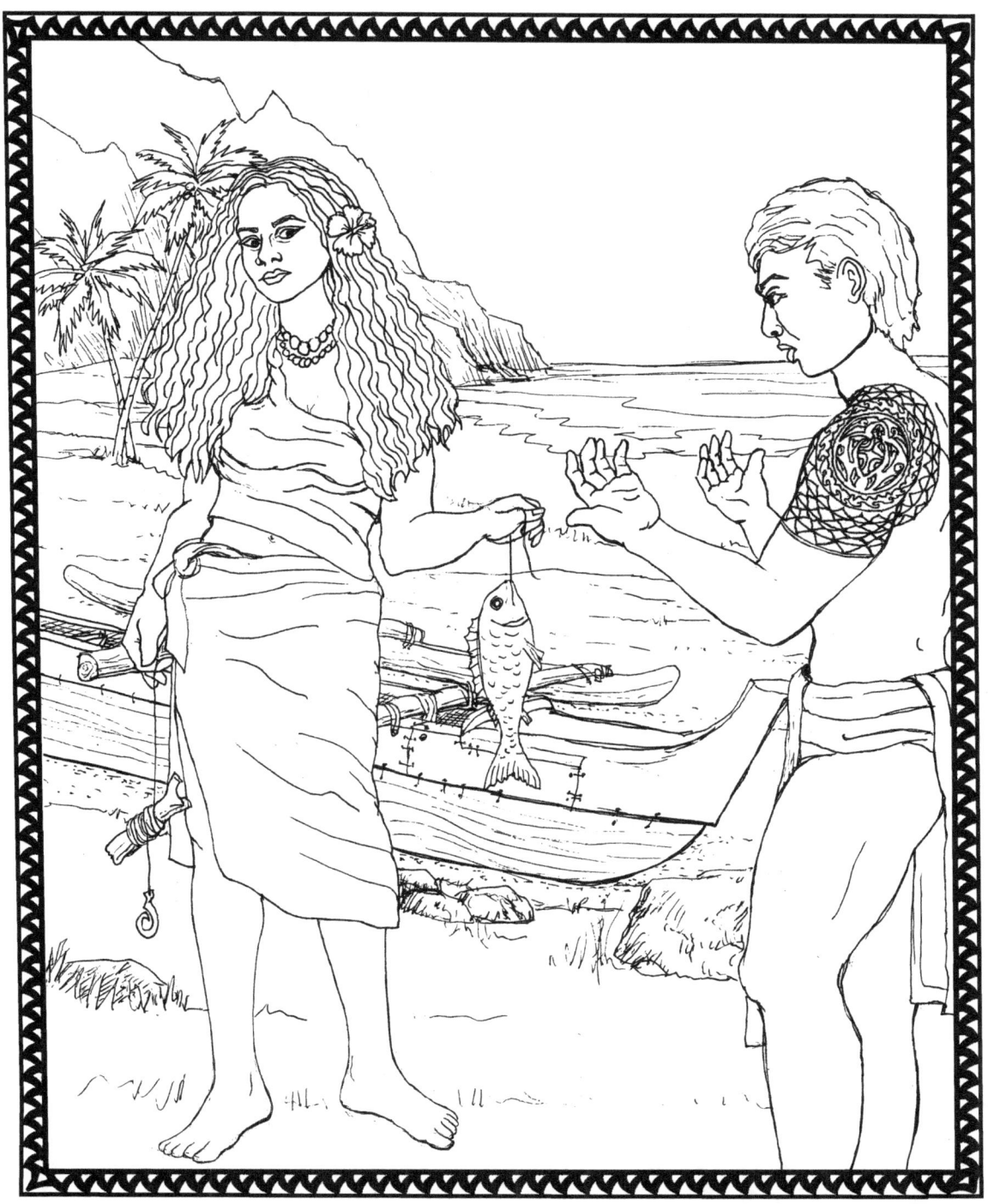
Keanahaki returned with only one small fish for Keawe.

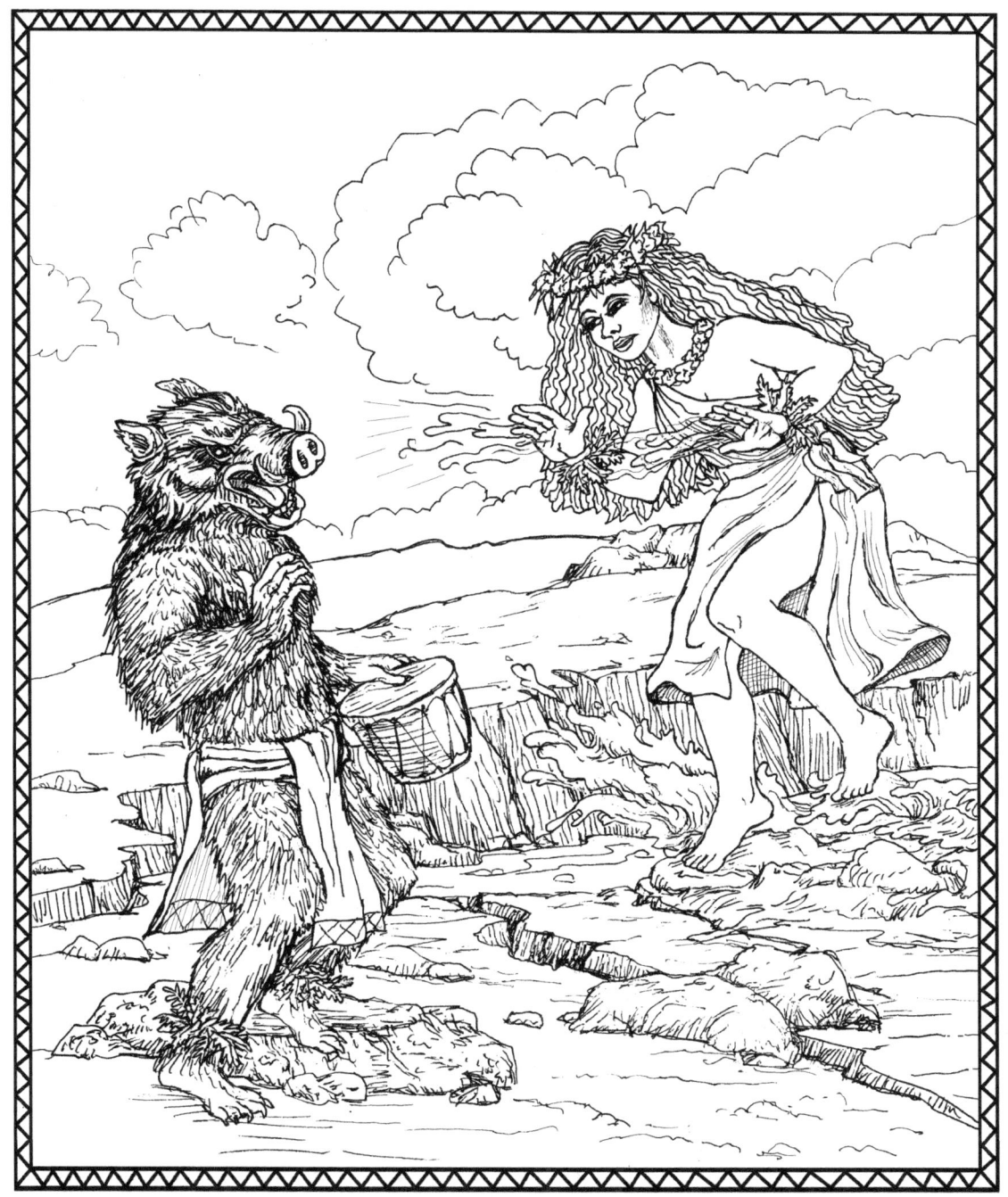

Pele started throwing lava at the Hog god.

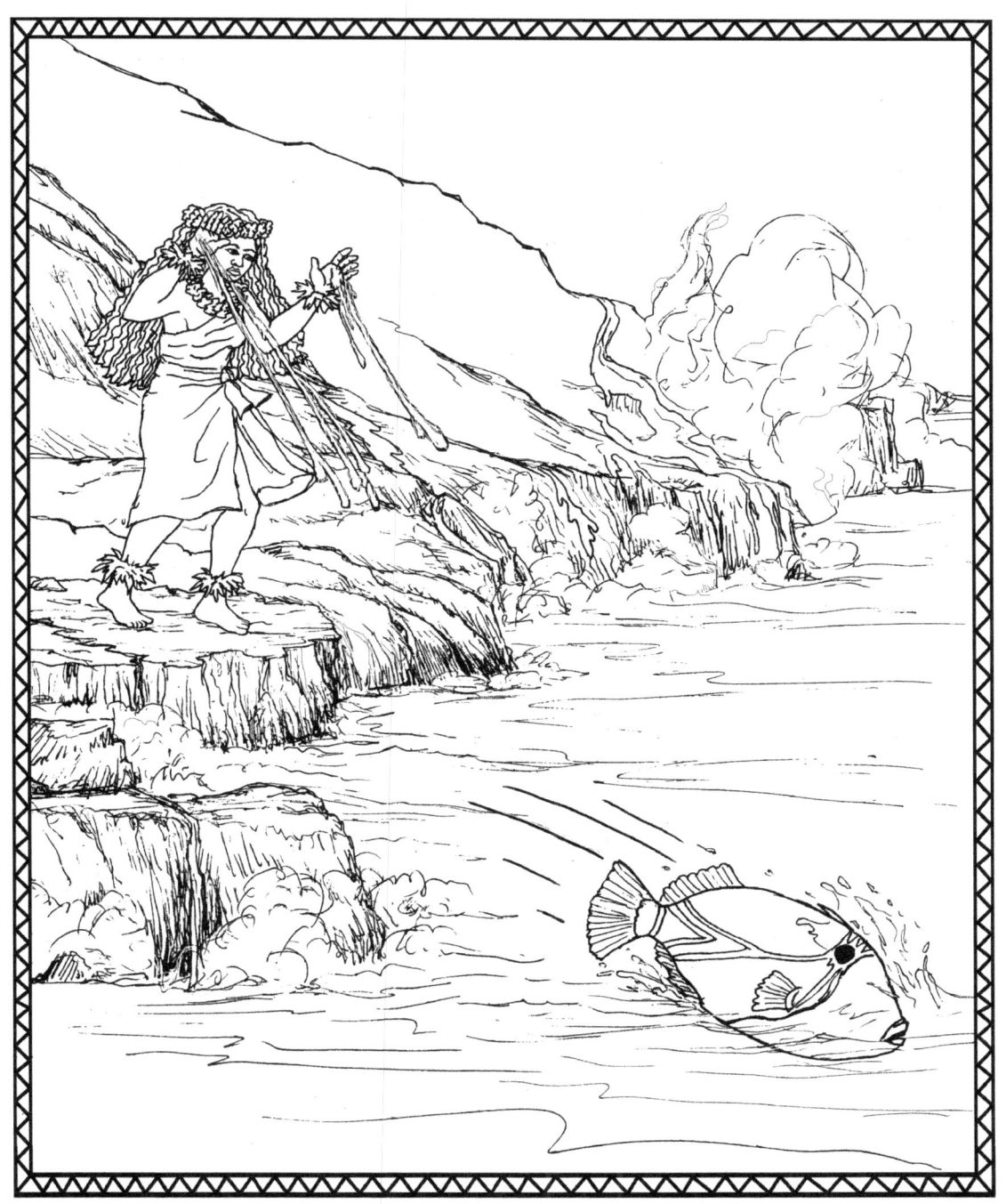

The Hog god turned into a Humuhumu to escape Pele's lava.

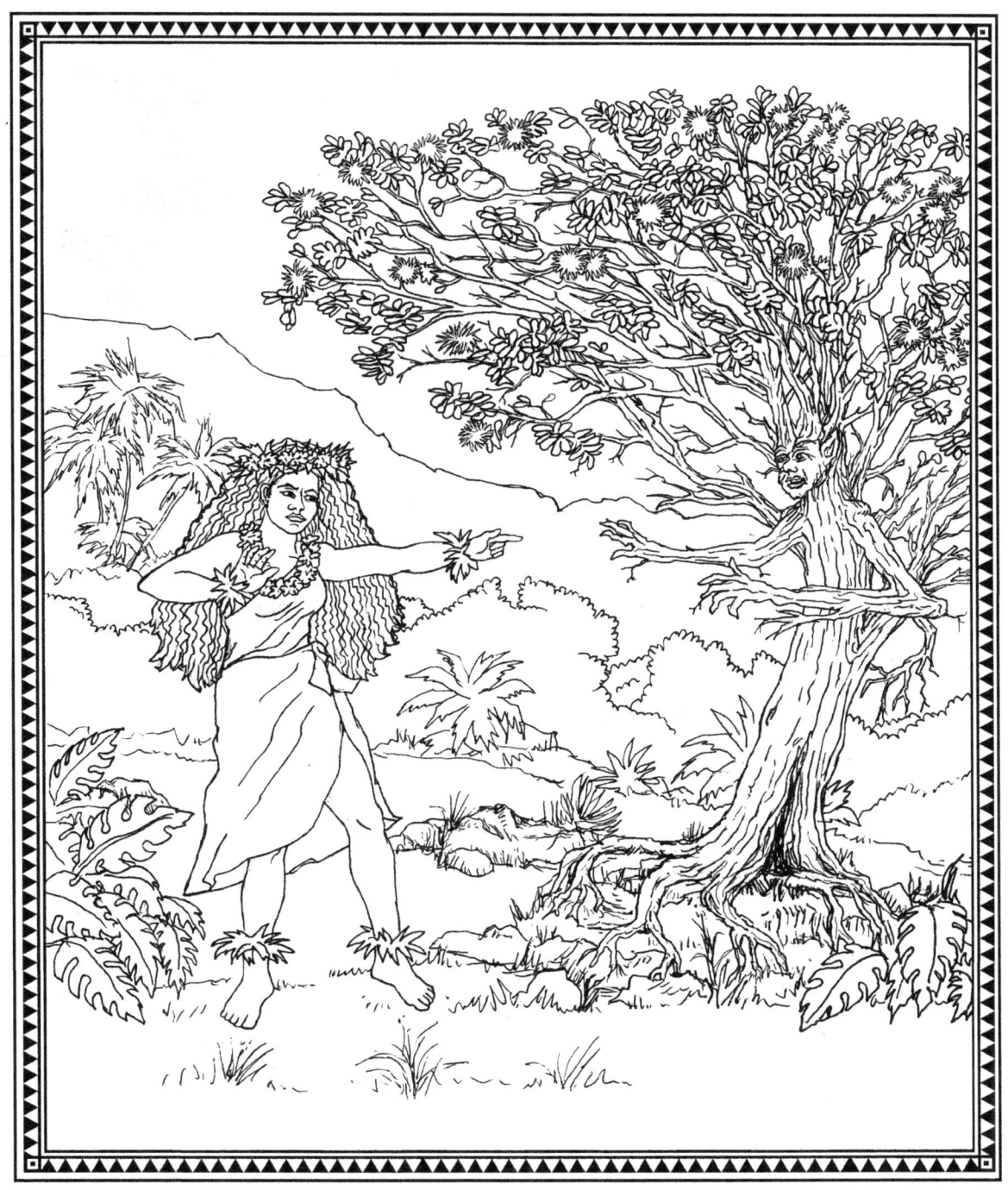
Pele changes Ohia into a misshapen tree.

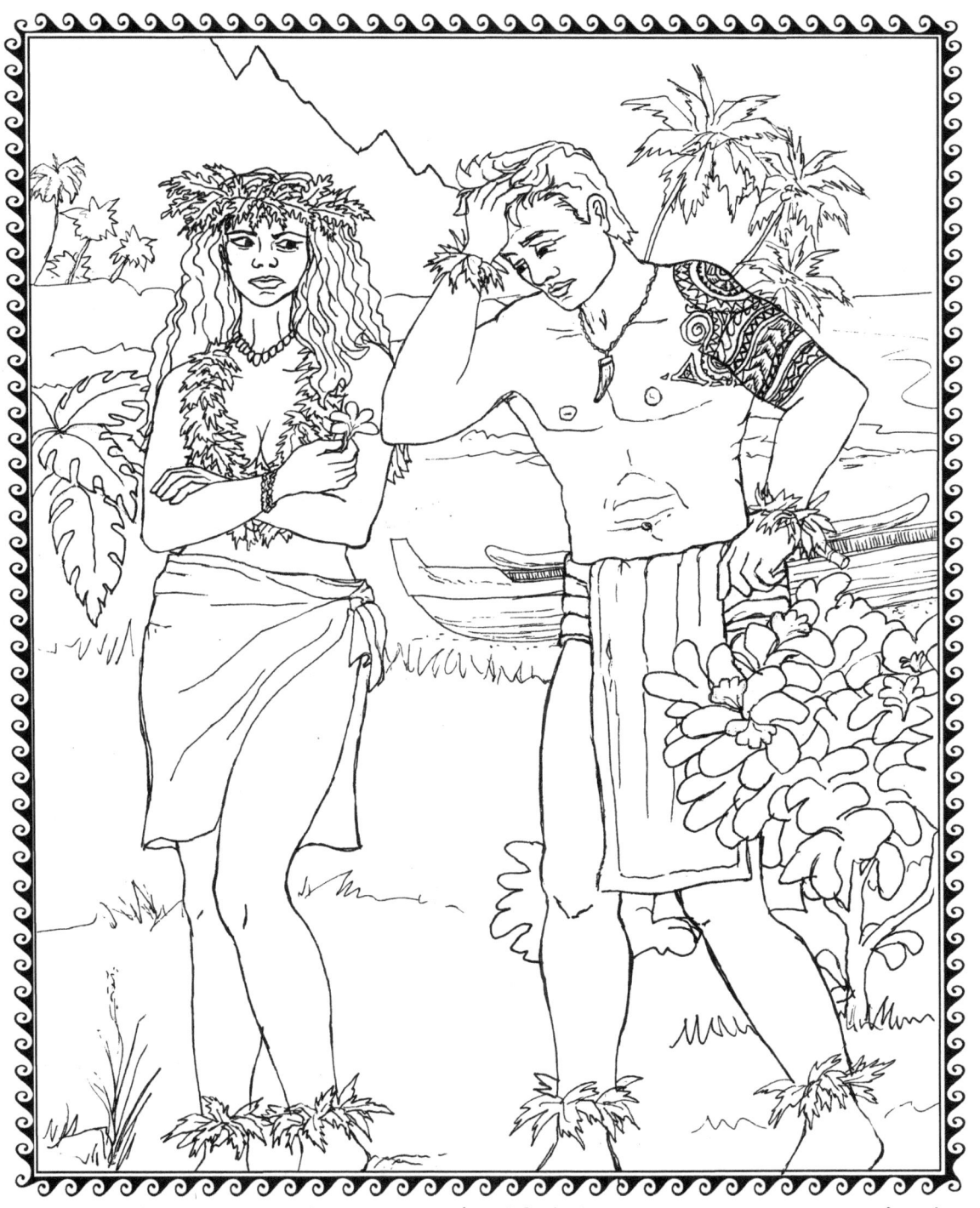

Naupaka gives Kauai a half blossom as a symbol.

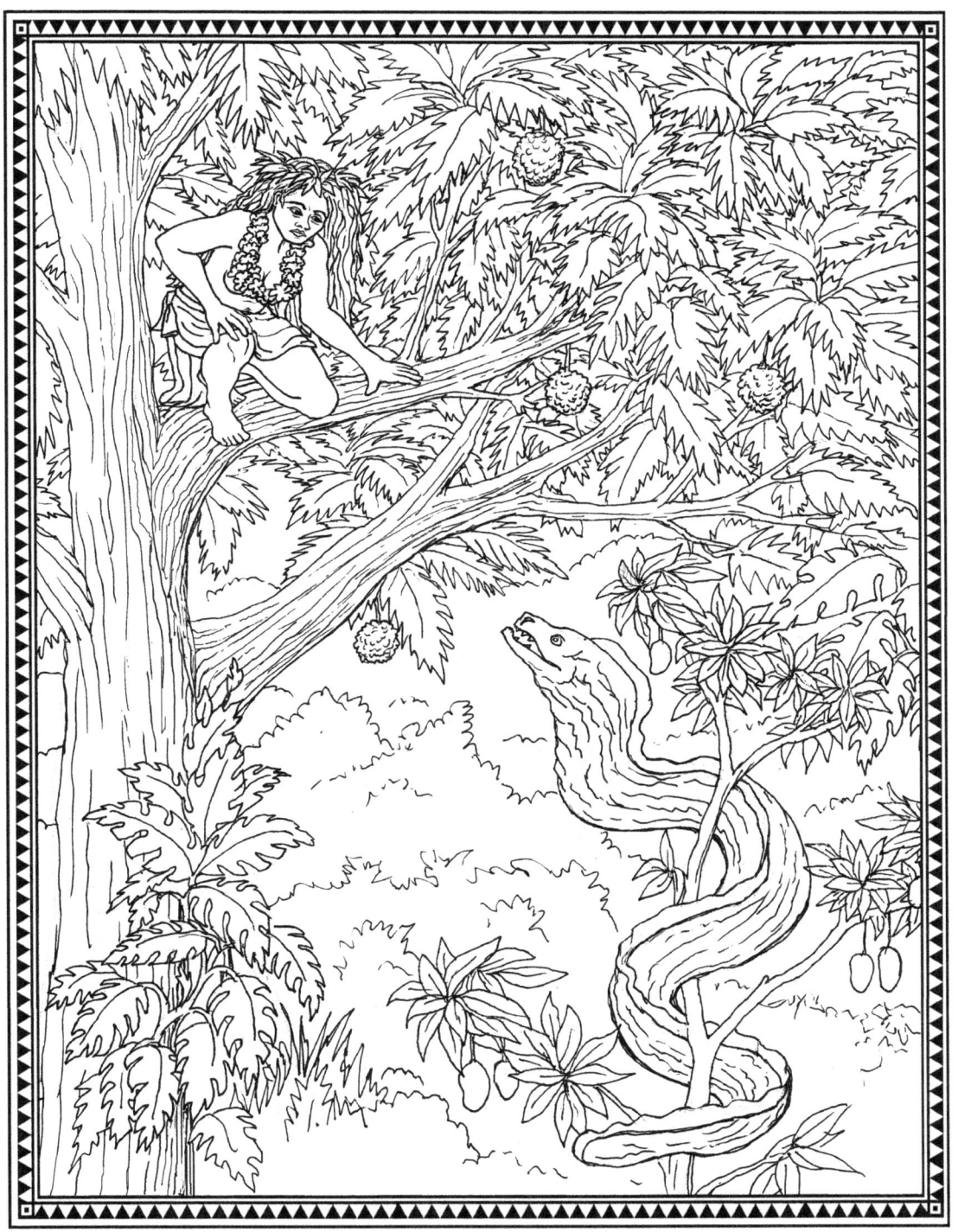

Hina escaping from Kuna Loa in the breadfruit tree.

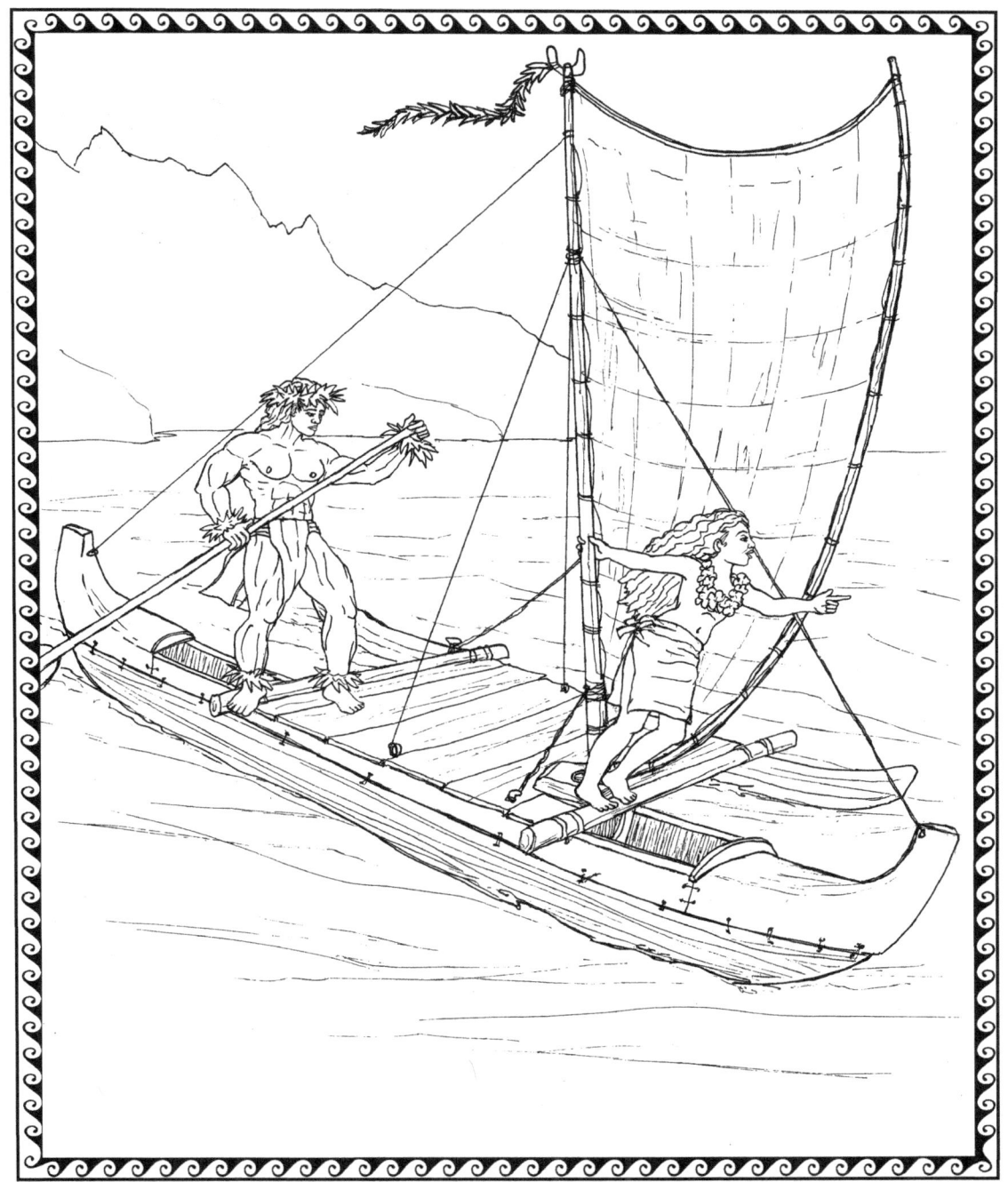

Maui teaches Moana way-finding.

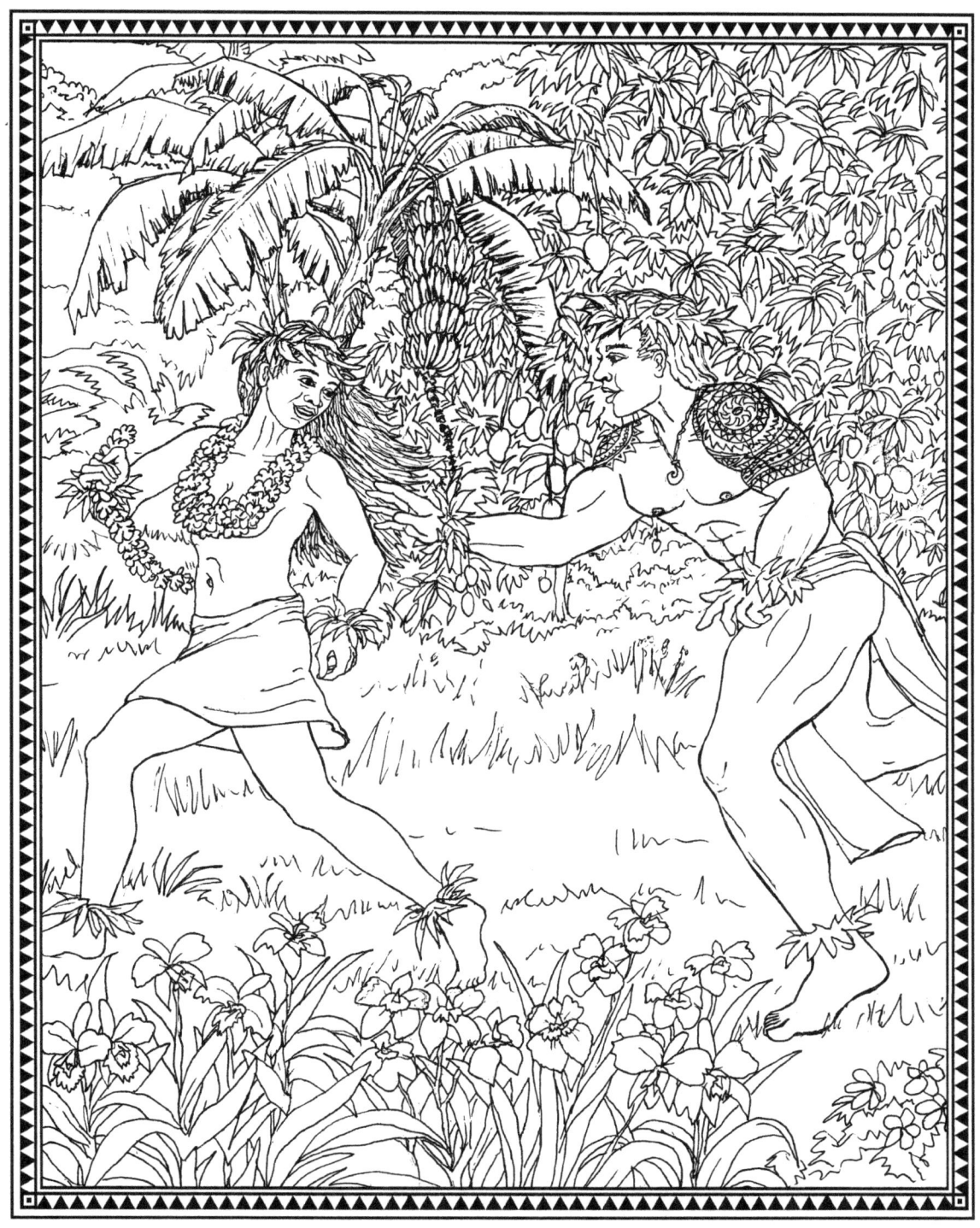

Maui chases Rau-kura through the swamp.

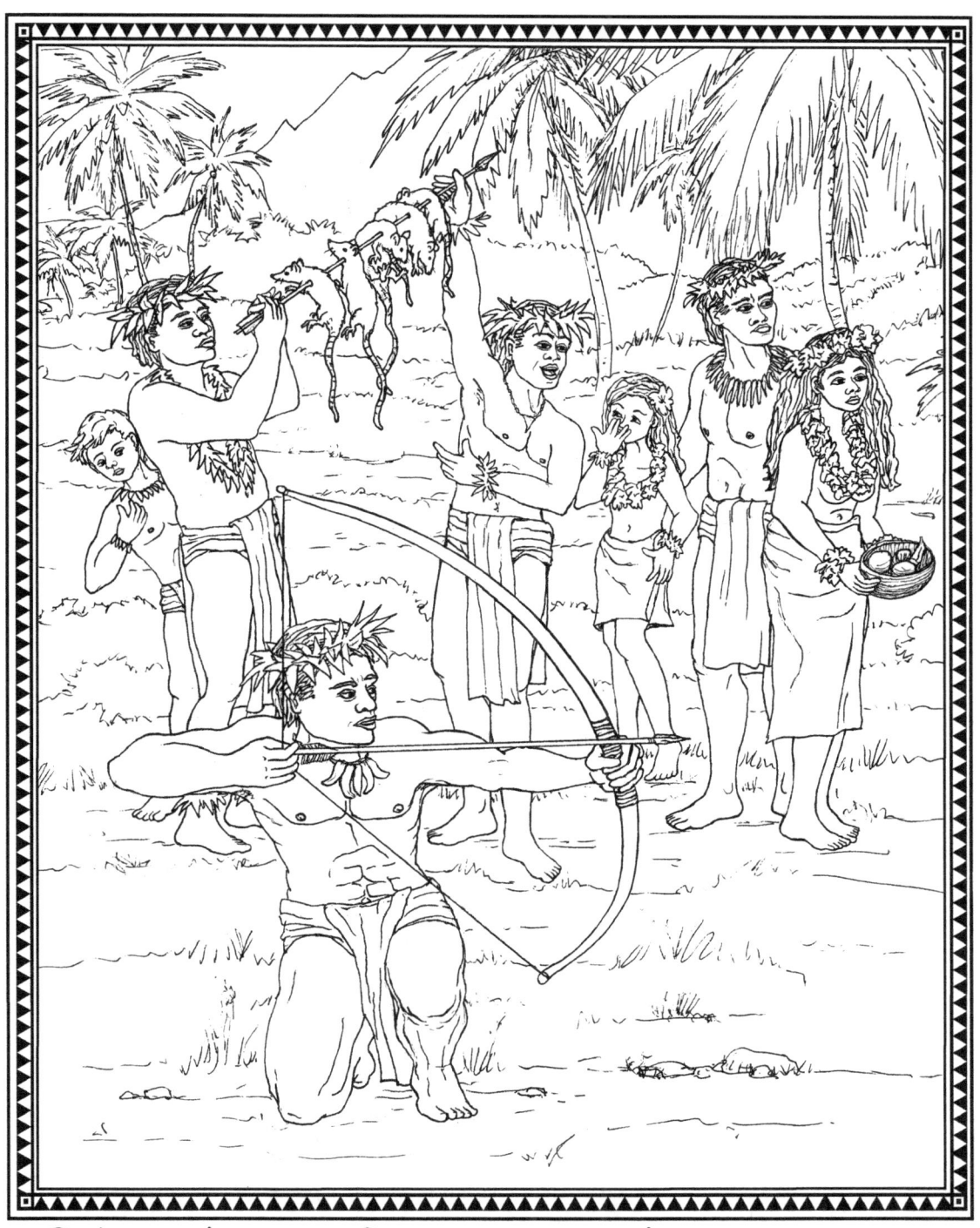
Piikoi shoots five rats with one arrow.

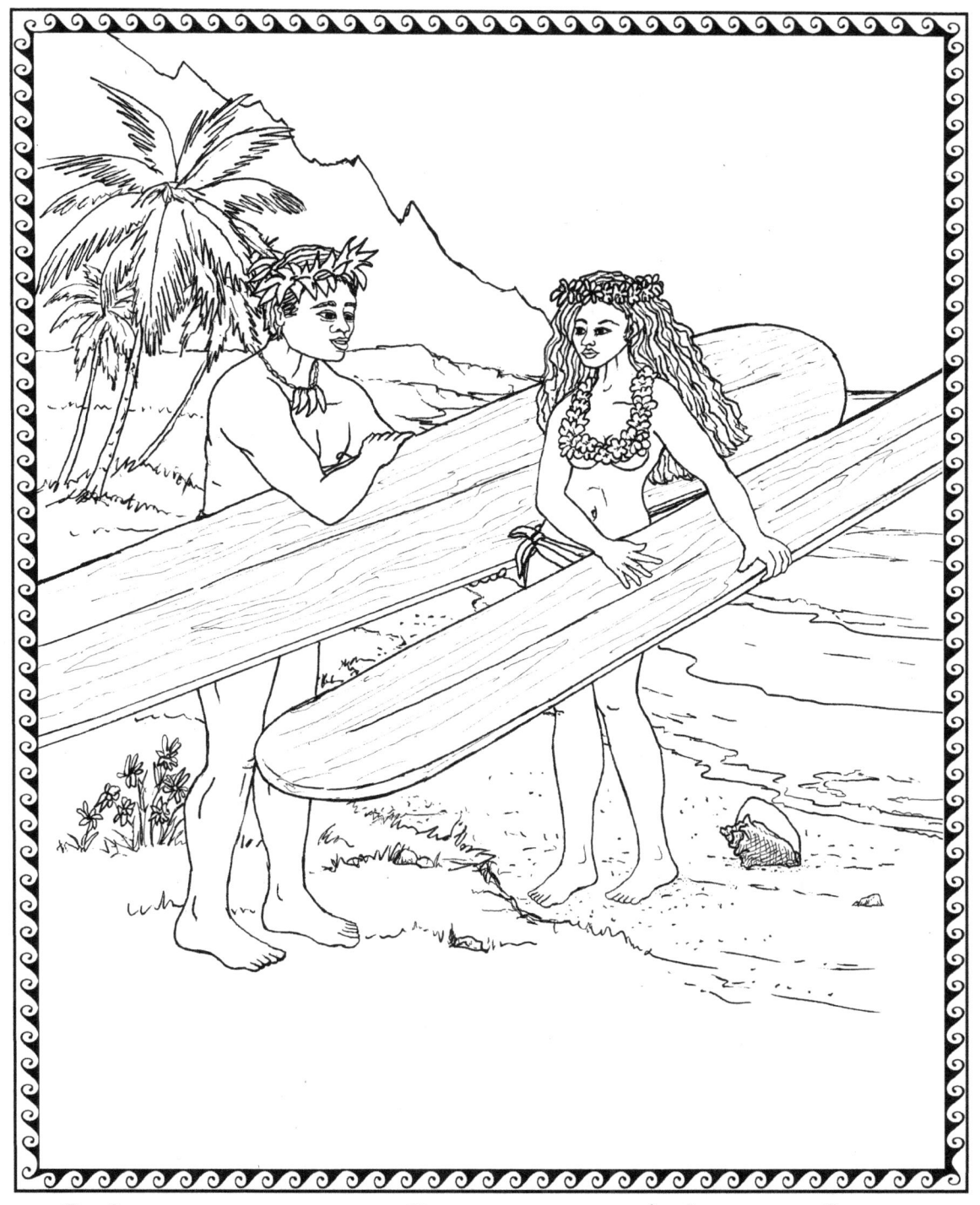
Piikoi meets a Princess while surfing.

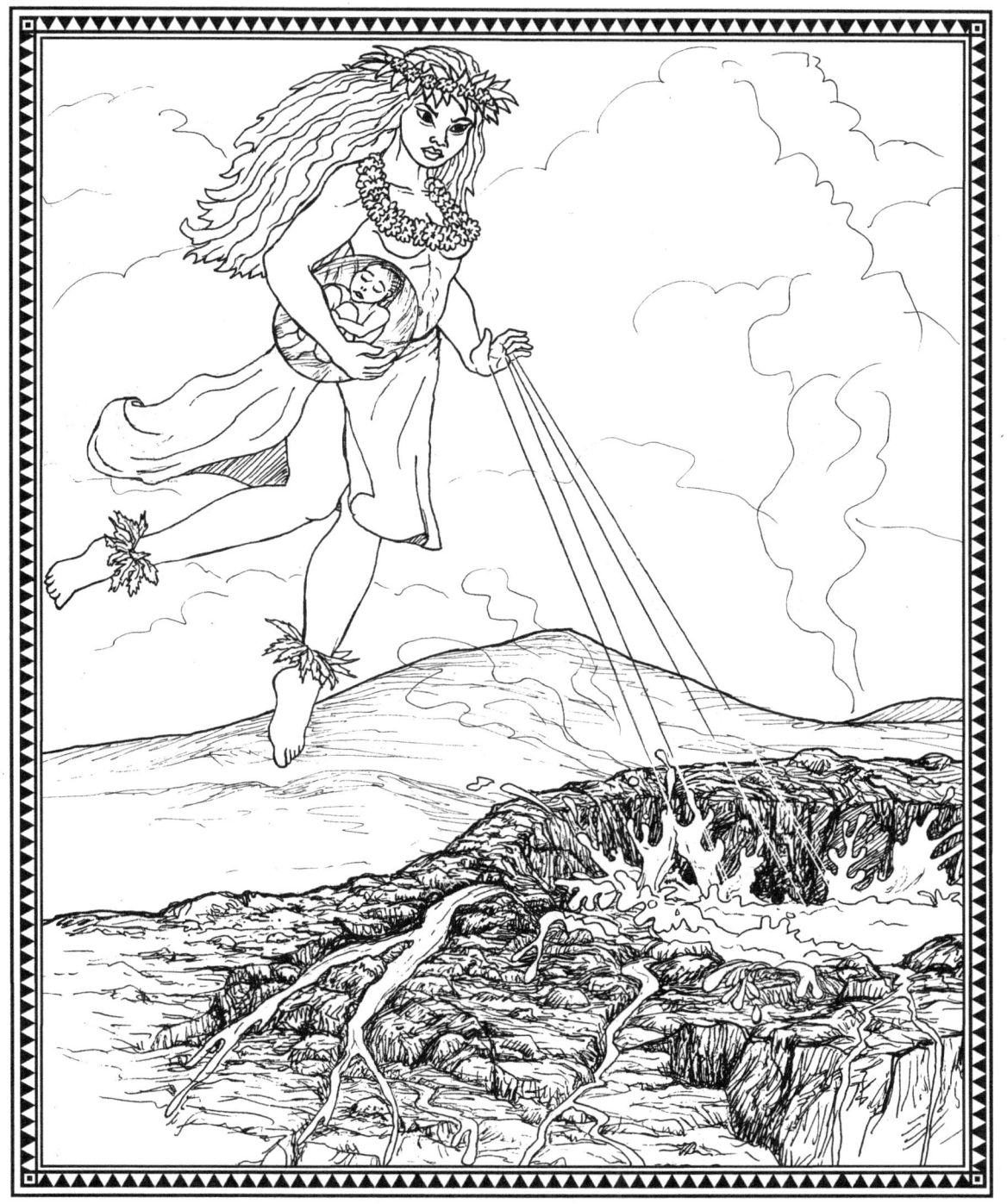

Pele carrying egg Hiiaka as she blasts a crater.

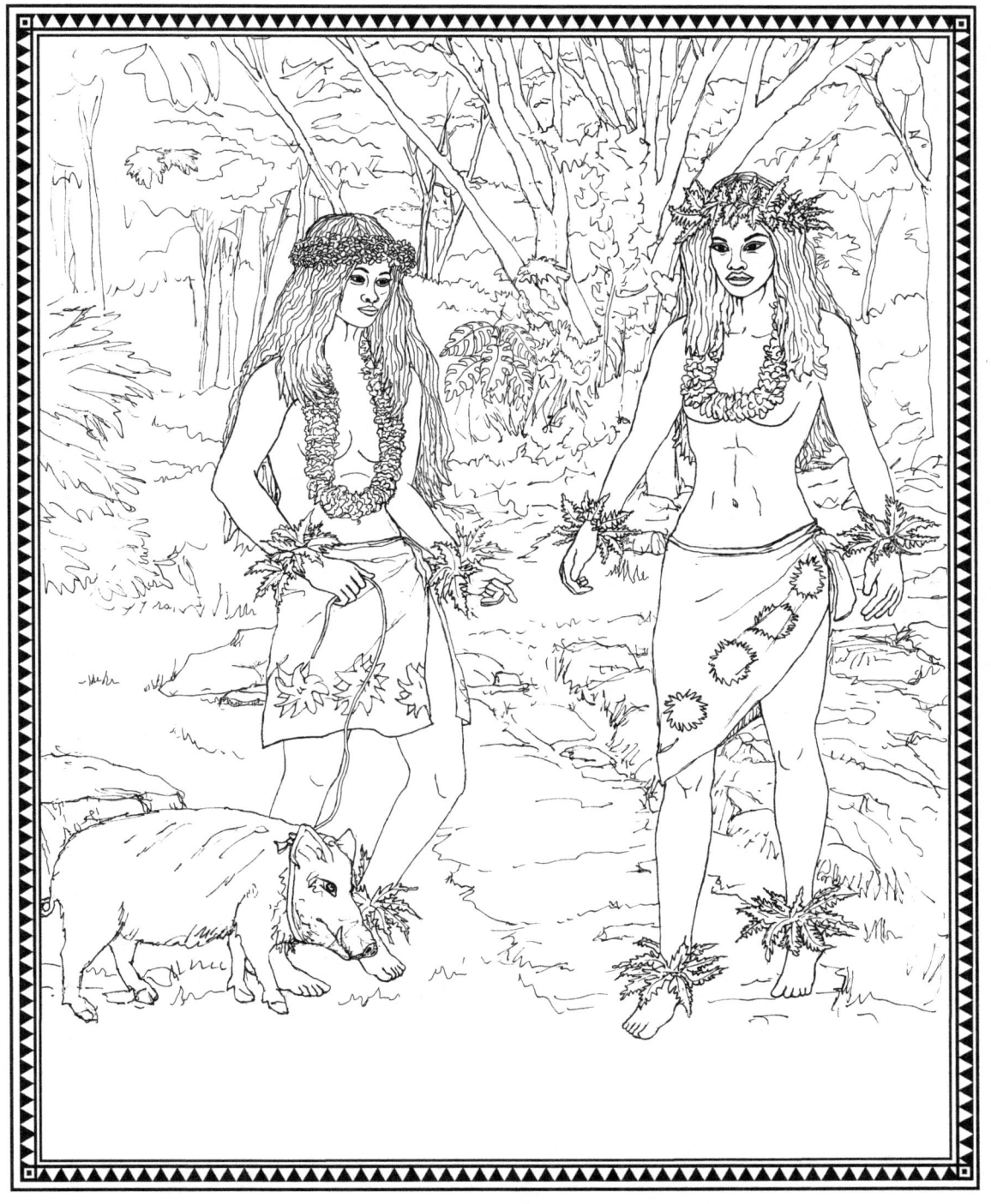

The Thrush Woman mistook Hiiaka for Pele.

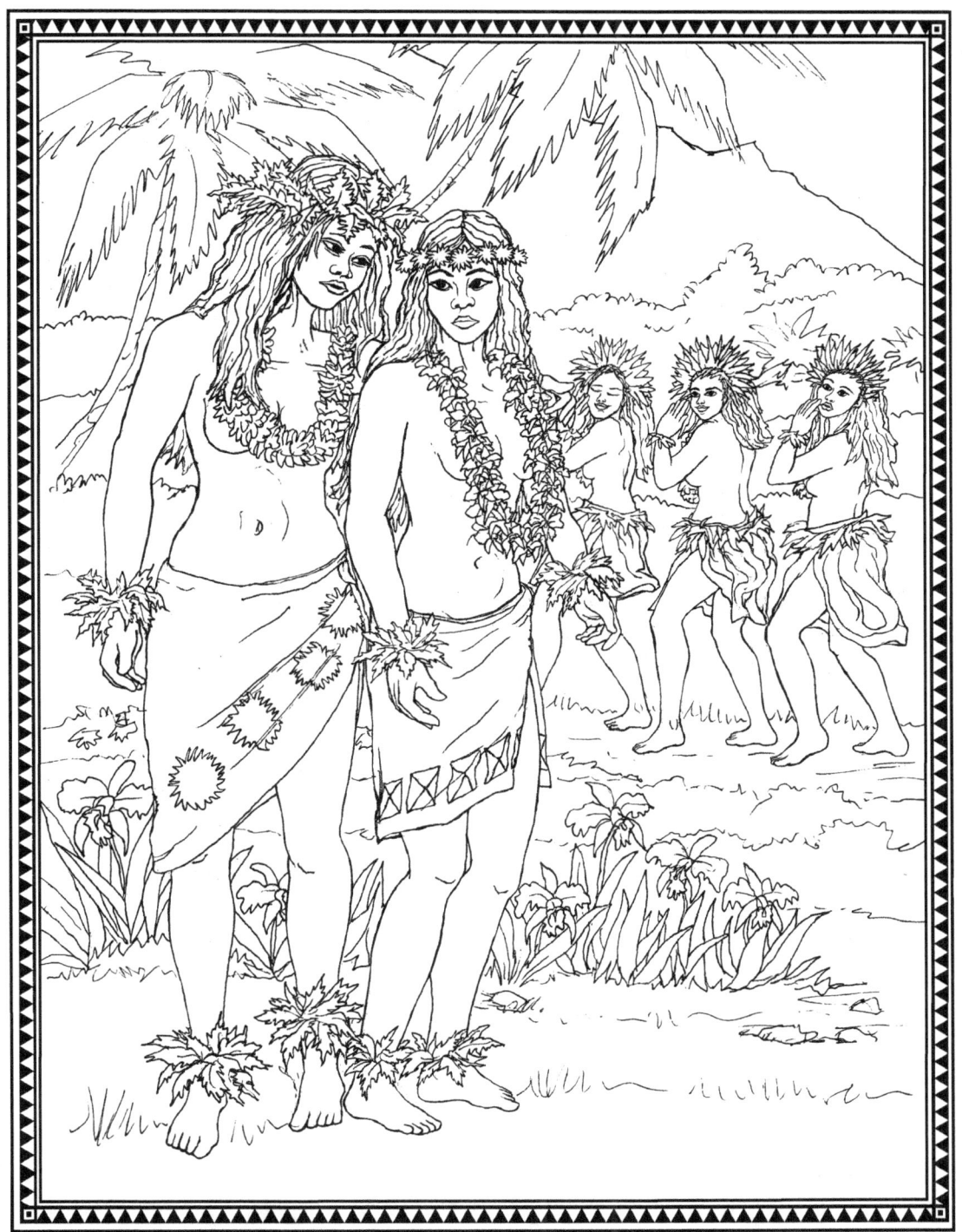

Hiiaka and her girlfriend Hopoi were great hula patrons.

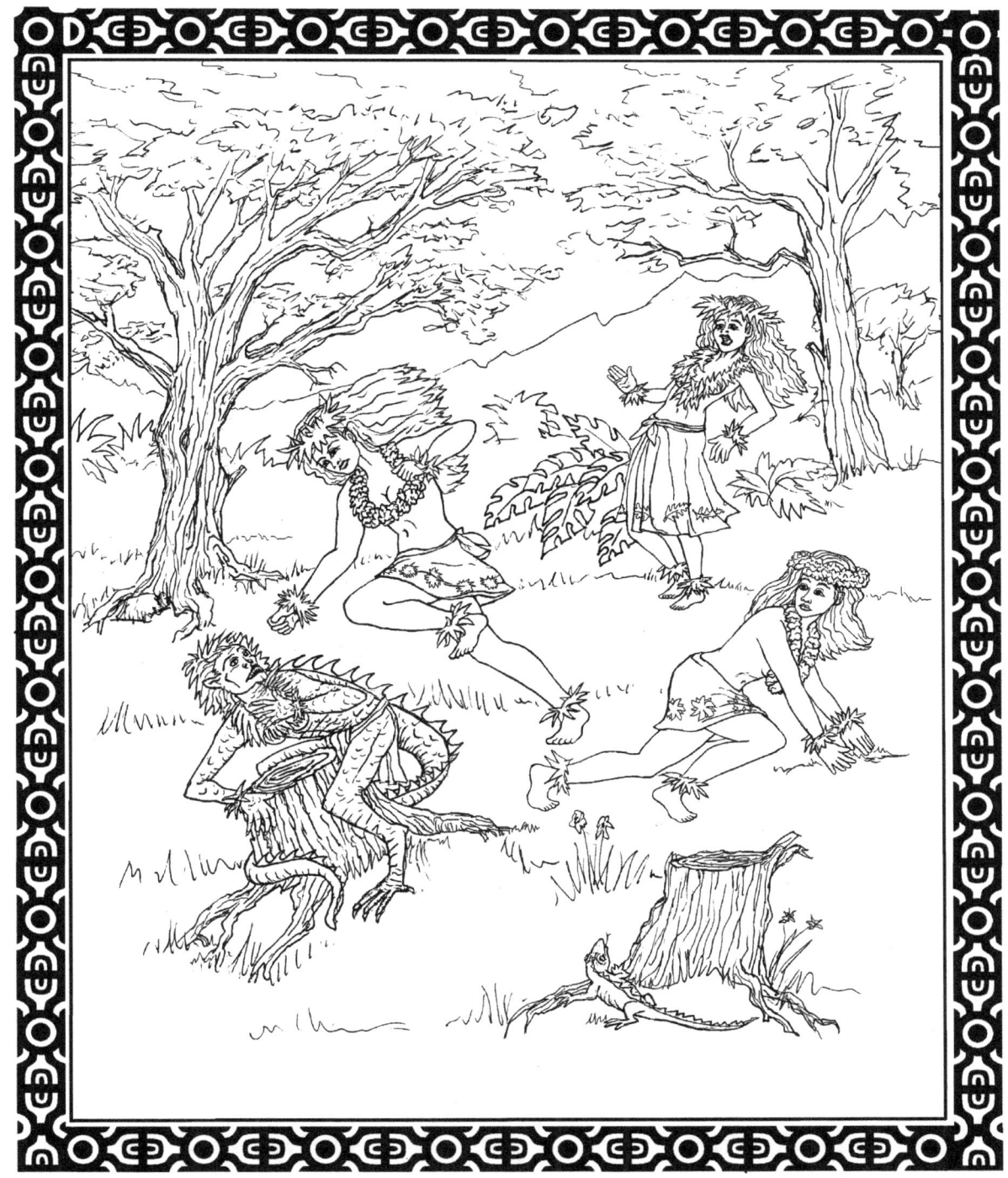

Hiiaka smashes a Mo'o woman disguised as a stump.

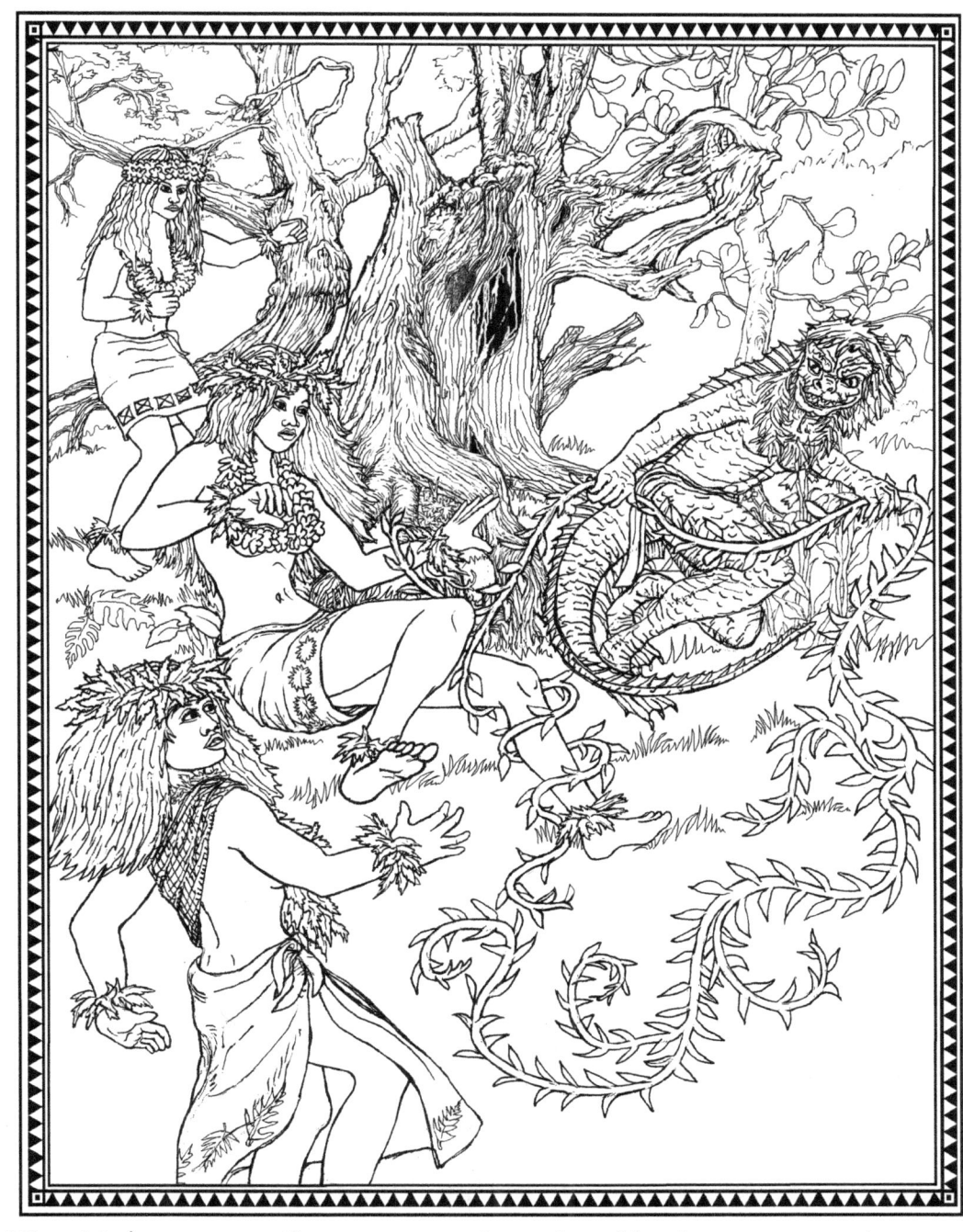

The Mo'o woman Panaewa entangles Hiiaka in an evil vine.

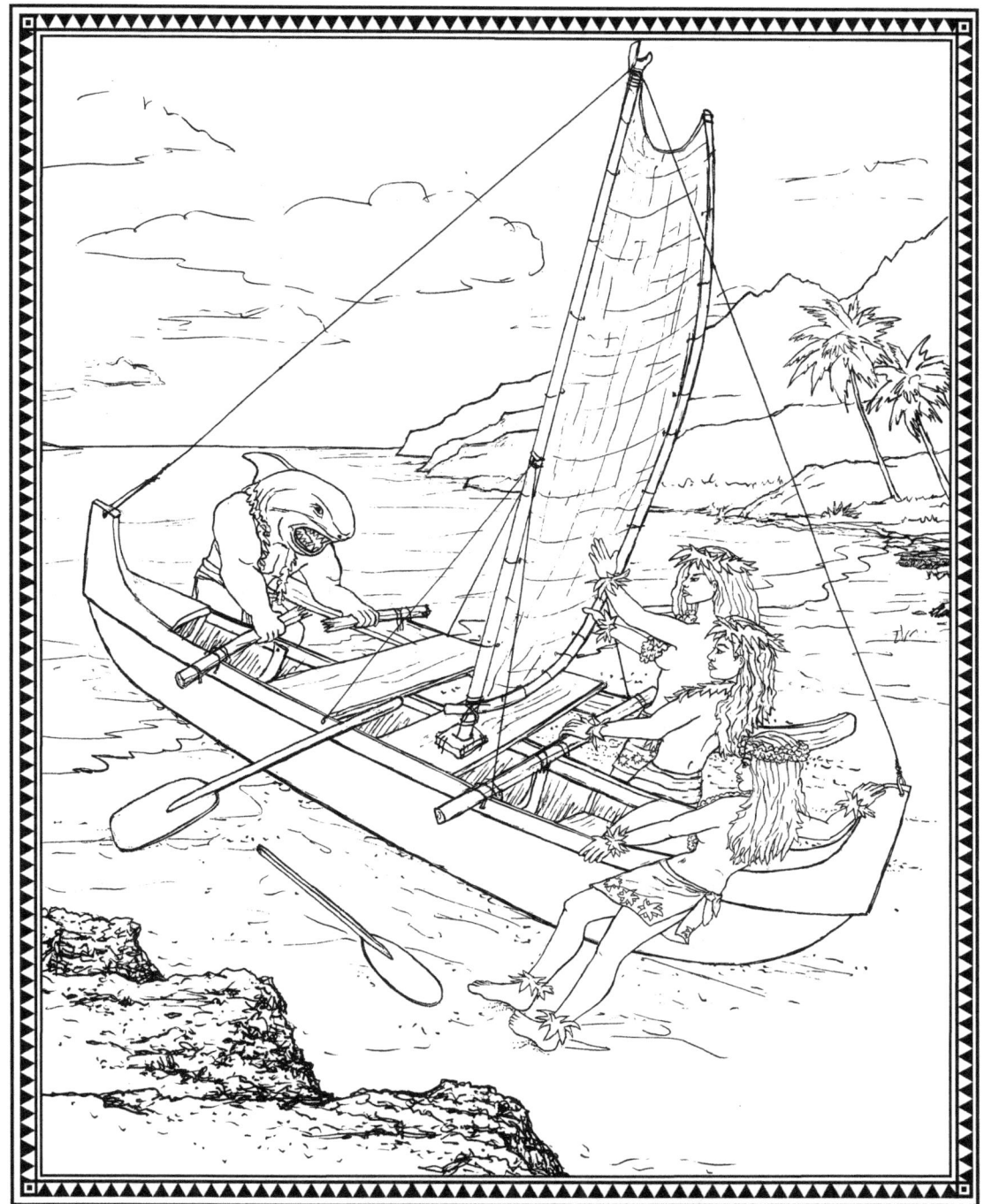

A sharkman attacked the three Wahine trying to sail to Maui.

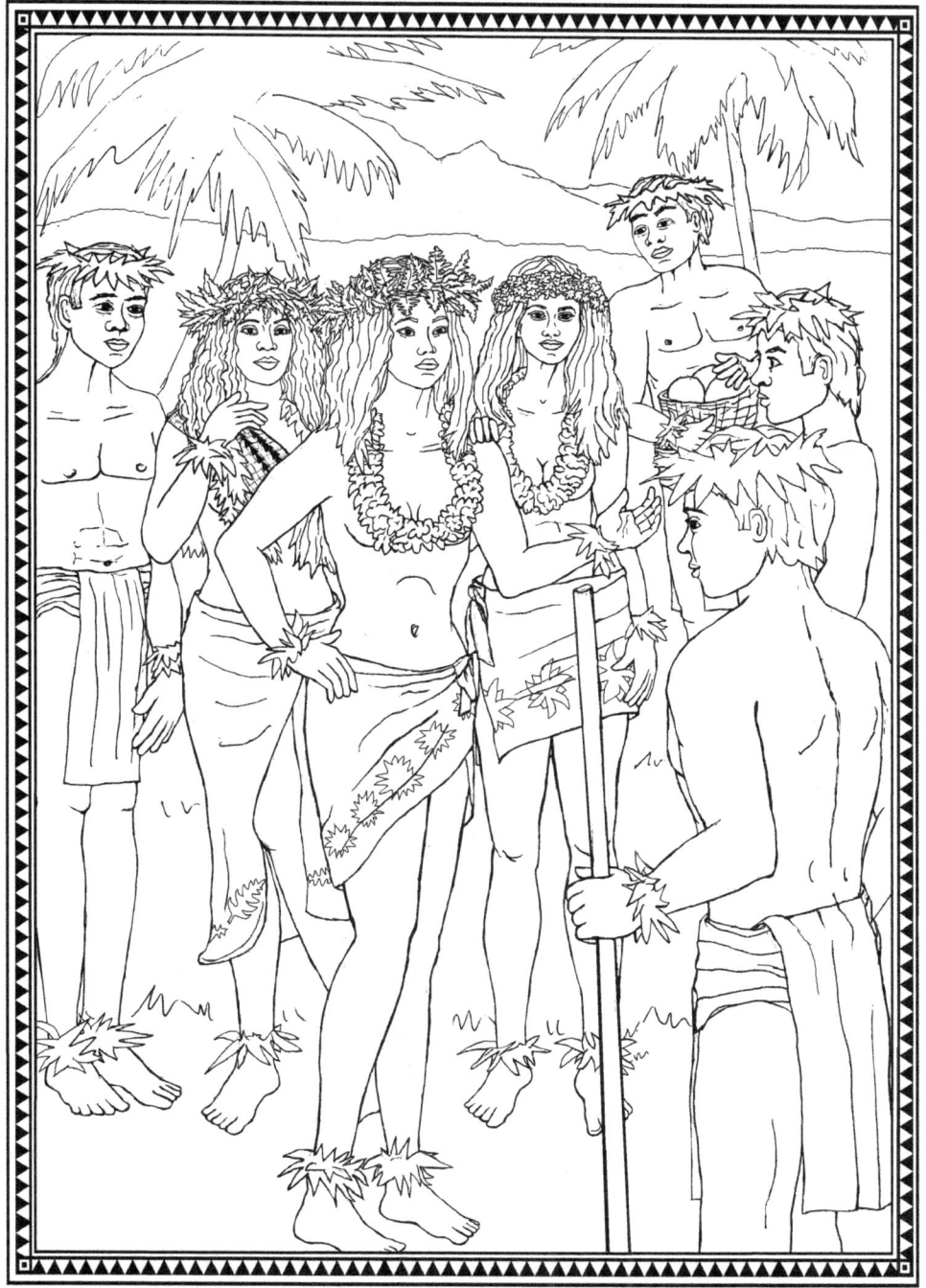

Men would gather around the 3 attractive Wahine.

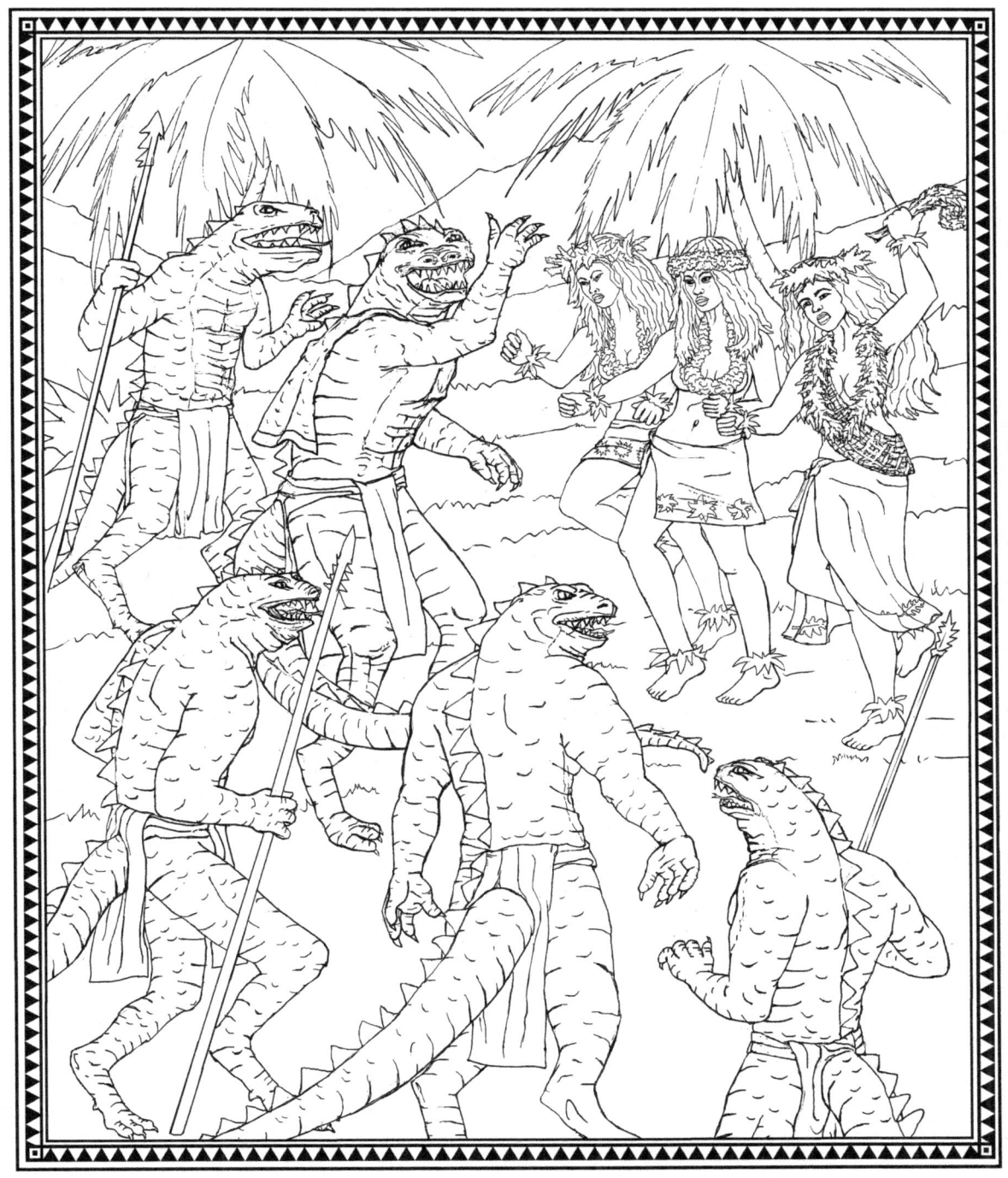

The demon-general orders his army to attack Hiiaka.

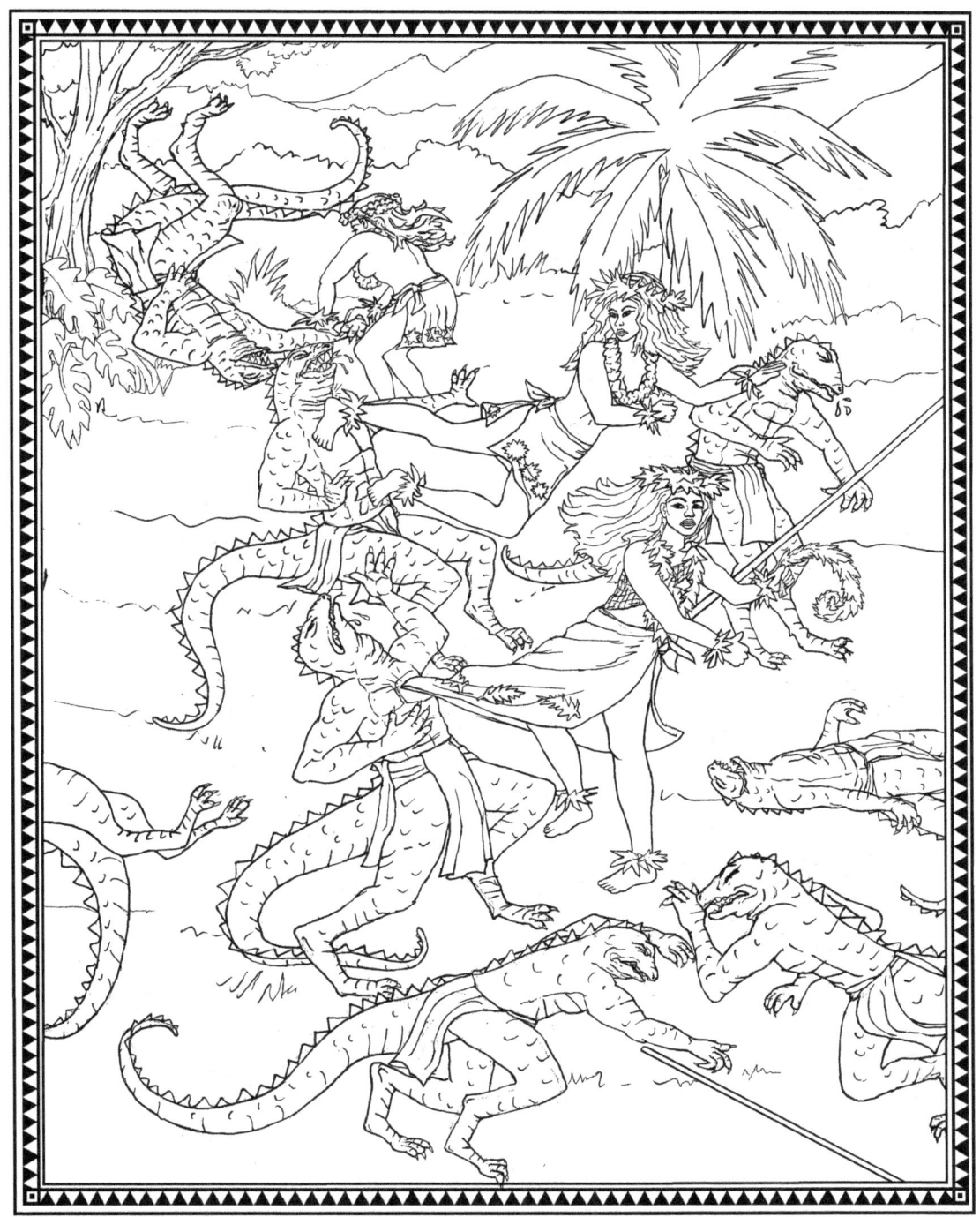
Leaping and slashing, the three wahine devastated the Mo'o army.

You can order large poster sized coloring pages of my designs from my website at Etsy.com Not only do I supply large sized images of the pages in this book, but images of Hawaiian scenes and even the Trump family from my other books. Make colorful posters for your room!

I have over a hundred large Hawaiian canvas prints and paintings, and nearly 200 smaller watercolor/prints at my Etsy art site. The coloring book pages of my Hawaiian Scene coloring books are based on some of these paintings. If you like my Hawaiian art, check all of these out at hawaiiseascapes.etsy.com

Check out my other books at Amazon. I have these books currently published:

Romantic and Fairy Tale Vintage Illustrations II an Adult Coloring Book
Old time ink and woodcut illustrations.

The Making of Romantic and Fairy Tale Vintage Illustrations an Illustrated Book for Adults
The description and illustration of each page above. How I redid old time ink and woodcut illustrations.

Achieve Success Coloring, a Subliminal Coloring Book for Adults
Set your mind for success while coloring.

The Making of Achieve Success Coloring, an Illustrated Book for Adults The inside story of using coloring to achieve success in general in life.

Find a Mate, a Subliminal Coloring Book for Adults
Adjust your mental thinking about finding your soul mate while coloring.

The Illustration of a Subliminal Book, About Using Coloring to Find Your Soul Mate The inside story of using subliminal coloring to find a mate

Lose Weight Coloring, A Subliminal Coloring Book for Adults
Make your weight loss easier while coloring subliminal messages.

The Making of Lose Weight Coloring, an Illustrated Book for Adults
The inside story of subliminal coloring weight loss with pictures of subliminal pages.

Make Money Coloring, A Subliminal Coloring Book for Adults
Enhance your money making abilities while coloring subliminal messages.

The Making of Make Money Coloring, an Illustrated book for Adults.
The inside story of how subliminal coloring works with pictures of subliminal pages.

Romantic and Fairy Tale Vintage Illustrations an Adult Coloring Book
Old time ink and woodcut illustrations.

The Making of Romantic and Fairy Tale Vintage Illustrations, an Illustrated Book for Adults The description and illustration of each page above.

The Making of Psychedelic Brain Freeze: An Illustrated Book for Adults
(explains the science behind optical illusions, shows how to color large poster sized pages to make your own art.)

The Making of Psychedelic Brain Freeze II: An Illustrated Book for Adults
(explains the science for more optical illusions, shows how to color large poster sized pages to make your own wall art.)

Relaxing Hawaiian Scenes, An Adult Coloring Book (first in the series)

Relaxing Hawaiian Scenes II, An Adult Coloring Book (2nd in the series)

The Making of Relaxing Hawaiian Scenes II, An Adult Illustrated Book

Relaxing Hawaiian Scenes III, An Adult Coloring Book (3rd in the series)

The Making of Relaxing Hawaiian Scenes III, An Adult Illustrated Book

Portraits of President Donald Trump and the First Family: an Adult Coloring Book (attractive personal pictures of all of President Trump's family)

Making of Portraits of President Donald Trump and the First Family, An Illustrated Book (explains some of the hidden Easter egg images in the drawings)

How to Import From China Starting With $250 and Make a Small Fortune!

Creation of the Universe and Other Strange Mormon Beliefs Revealed. (A church member tells all the Secrets the Authorities Don't Want to Talk About.)

How To Use Your Money Making Genes to Become a Success and Make a Small Fortune.

How to Publish Books on Amazon Kindle and Make a Small Fortune, The E-Book Money Making System

Thanks....

www.ingramcontent.com/pod-product-compliance
Lightning Source LLC
Chambersburg PA
CBHW062157220526
45470CB00009B/2846